Gems IN THE SMITHSONIAN

Gems IN THE SMITHSONIAN

Paul E. Desautels, Curator, Division of Mineralogy

SMITHSONIAN INSTITUTION PRESS   WASHINGTON, D.C.   1972

Designed by Elizabeth Sur

Photography by Lee Boltin: cover; frontispiece;
pages 6, 11, 19 center, 20, 21 top, 29, 31, 32, 40 bottom,
43, 45 top, 48, 49 bottom, 52, 53, 55, 56 top

Color separations by Case-Hoyt Corp., Rochester,
New York; lithography by American Lithograph
Division of Case-Hoyt Corp., Atlanta, Georgia

Library of Congress Cataloging in Publication Data

Desautels, Paul E.
   Gems in the Smithsonian.
   1965 ed. issued under title: Gems in the Smithsonian
Institution.
   1. Gems. 2. Smithsonian Institution. I. Title.
NK5510.W3D4   1972   736.2'074'0153   76-39489
ISBN O-87474-117-3
ISBN O-87474-121-1 (pbk.)

*Cover: one of the more important gifts to the
Smithsonian gem collection in recent years
is the 423-carat Logan Sapphire. Given by
Mrs. John A. Logan, this dazzling Ceylon sapphire,
set with 20 diamonds, is most likely the largest
gem of this coveted rich blue color known.*

*Frontispiece: faceted, egg-shaped, 7000-carat
rock crystal from Brazil. The gold stand is
inset mostly with Montana sapphires. The gem
was cut and the stand was designed and
constructed by John Sinkankas of California.*

Contents

The Hall of Gems, which houses the
National Collection of Gems in the
National Museum of Natural History.

A special vault housing the Eugenie
Blue Diamond (page 29), and two
other cases in the Hall of Gems.

The
National
Gem
Collection

Man has been using certain mineral species for personal adornment since prehistoric times. However, of the almost 2000 different mineral species, relatively few, perhaps only 100, have been used traditionally as gems. To be useful as a gem, a mineral species should have durability as well as beauty. Lack of durability eliminates most minerals as gems, although some relatively fragile gem materials such as opal are prized because of their exceptional beauty. Actually, some gem materials are not minerals at all. Pearl, amber, jet, and coral, unlike true minerals, are formed by living organisms.

In the National Gem Collection, the Smithsonian Institution has assembled a large representation of all known gem materials. The display portion of the collection consists of more than 1000 items selected to illustrate the various kinds of gems and to show how their beauty is enhanced by cutting and polishing. Most of these gems are gifts of public-spirited donors who, by giving the gems directly or by establishing endowments for their purchase, have contributed to the enjoyment of the many thousands of persons who visit the Smithsonian Institution each week.

The National Gem Collection had its beginning in 1884 when Prof. F. W. Clarke, then honorary curator of the Division of Mineralogy, prepared an exhibit of American precious stones as a part of the Smithsonian Institution's display at the New Orleans Exposition. The same collection was displayed at the Cincinnati Exposition the following year. Between 1886 and 1890 the growth of the collection was slow, but in 1891 most of the precious stones collected by Dr. Joseph Leidy of Philadelphia were obtained. Combined

Professor F. W. Clarke, former honorary curator who assembled the Smithsonian Institution's first gem collection in 1884.

Dr. Isaac Lea, Philadelphia gem collector whose collection was the nucleus around which the gem collection has been built through the years.

Dr. Leander T. Chamberlain, son-in-law of Dr. Isaac Lea. He became honorary curator of the gem collection in 1897. Income from his bequest is used to purchase gems for the Isaac Lea gem collection.

with those already on hand, all were exhibited at the World's Columbian Exposition at Chicago in 1893.

Great stimulus was given the collection in 1894 when Mrs. Frances Lea Chamberlain bequeathed the precious stones assembled by her father, Dr. Isaac Lea. Her husband, Dr. Leander T. Chamberlain, who in 1897 became honorary curator of the collection, contributed a large number of specimens and, upon his death, left an endowment fund. The income from that fund has been used to steadily increase the collection over the years. Extremely rare and costly gems suitable for exhibition are beyond the income derived from the Chamberlain endowment, but this gap has been filled by many important donations, the most notable being the gift in 1959 of the Hope Diamond by Harry Winston, Inc., New York City. Thus, from modest beginnings in 1884, there has been accumulated the magnificent collection of gems belonging to the people of the United States. The collection is displayed in the Smithsonian Institution's great National Museum of Natural History.

The
Study
of
Gems

To the average person it might seem that a jeweler's showcase of gems presents innumerable kinds of precious stones, when actually only a few species of minerals are there. Perhaps only diamond, ruby, emerald, aquamarine, sapphire, opal, tourmaline, and amethyst would comprise the entire stock. Yet, since the mineral kingdom consists of somewhat less than 2000 distinct species, it would seem that a few more kinds of gemstones would be available. Certainly, many more minerals than are seen displayed by the jeweler have been used as gems over the centuries. The study of all these species of gem minerals constitutes modern gemology—a specialized branch of the science of mineralogy.

With the few exceptions already noted, all gems are minerals found in the Earth's crust. A mineral is a natural substance having a definite chemical composition and definite physical characteristics by which it can be recognized. However, for a mineral to qualify as a gem it must meet at least some of the accepted requirements—brilliance, beauty, durability, rarity, and portability. Of course, if a gemstone happens to be "fashionable" it will have additional importance. Rarely does a single gem possess all of these qualities. A fine-quality diamond, having a high degree of brilliance and fire, together with extreme hardness and great rarity, comes closest to this ideal, and in the world of western fashion the diamond is unchallenged among gems. The opal, by contrast, is relatively fragile, and it depends mainly on its rarity and its beautiful play of colors to be considered gem material.

When a gem material, as found in nature, has at least a minimum number of necessary qualities, it is then the task of the lapidary, or gem cutter, to cut it and polish it in such a way to take greatest advantage of all its possibilities for beauty and adornment.

PHYSICAL CHARACTERISTICS OF GEMSTONES

When a gemologist or a gem cutter examines an unworked mineral fragment (called *rough*) he looks for certain distinguishing characteristics that will aid him in identifying the mineral and in determining the procedures he should use in cutting it.

It is difficult to list these characteristics in the order of importance, but *hardness* would rank high. Hardness of a gem is best defined as its resistance to abrasion or scratching. Most commonly used for comparison is the Mohs scale, which consists of selected common minerals arranged in the order of increasing hardness. On this scale, topaz is rated as 8 in hardness, ruby as 9, and diamond, the hardest known substance, as 10. Any gem with a hardness less than that of quartz, number 7 in the scale, is unlikely to be sufficiently scratch-resistant for use as a gem. A less precise scale, using common objects for comparison, might include the fingernail with a hardness up to 2½, a copper coin up to 3, a knife blade to 5½, a piece of window glass at about 5½, and a steel file between 6 and 7, depending on the type of steel. By this scale, any stone that remains unmarred after being scraped by a piece of window glass will have a hardness greater than 5½. The more important gemstones—which include diamond, ruby, sapphire, and emerald—all have a hardness much greater than 5½.

The size of a gemstone usually is indicated by its *weight* in *carats*. The expression "a 10-carat stone" has meaning—if somewhat inexact—even to the nonexpert. Specifically, a carat is one-fifth of a gram, which is a unit of weight in the metric system small enough so that approximately 28 grams make an ounce. A 140-carat gemstone, then, weighs about an ounce.

Another distinguishing characteristic of a gemstone is its *specific gravity*, which is an expression of the relationship between the stone's own weight and the weight of an equal volume of water. We are aware of a difference in weight when we compare lead and wood, yet it would not always be correct to say that lead weighs more than wood, for a large piece of wood can weigh more than a small piece of lead. Only by comparing equal volumes of these materials can the extent of the weight difference be clear and unmistakable. Diamond is 3½ times heavier than the same volume of water, so its specific gravity is 3½. Since each species of gem has its own specific gravity, which can easily be determined without harming the stone, this standard of comparison is a valuable aid in identifying gems. Several techniques have been devised for determining specific gravity, and most of them make use of some kind of weighing device or balance.

MOHS SCALE OF HARDNESS

Soft

Talc—1
Gypsum—2
Calcite—3
Fluorite—4
Apatite—5
Feldspar—6
Quartz—7
Topaz—8
Corundum—9
Diamond—10

Hard

Sketch of a simple balance used to determine specific gravity of a gemstone. The operator places the gemstone in the upper pan (A), moves the weight (B) along the beam (C) until it balances perfectly, and notes the number at the weight's position. He then transfers the gemstone to the lower pan (D), which is completely immersed in water, and moves the weight along the beam to restore balance. He notes the scale number at the new position and determines the specific gravity simply by dividing the first number by the difference between the two numbers. If the gemstone is large, the operator can use heavier sliding weights (E).

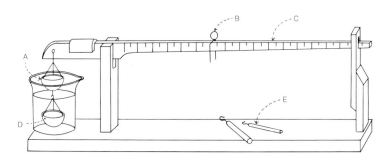

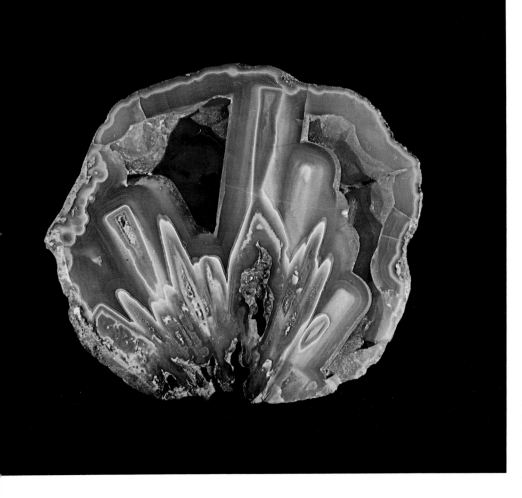

Various shades of brown and red in agate, as in this polished specimen from Chihuahua, Mexico, indicate the presence of traces of iron impurities.

A chrysoberyl cat's-eye ring. The bright band of reflected light arises from thousands of needlelike inclusions in parallel arrangement within the stone.

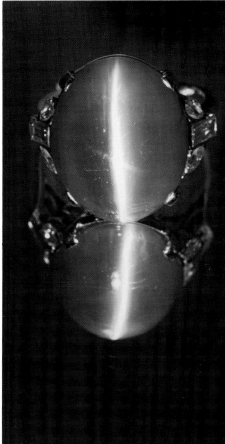

Among the most striking and useful of the distinguishing characteristics of gemstones are those that involve their effects on light.

An important effect of a gem on light is the production of color, upon which many gems depend for their beauty. Some gem materials, such as lapis lazuli, have little to offer except color. Many of the major gem minerals vary widely in color, owing to the presence of finely dispersed impurities in extremely small quantities. Traces of iron in the composition of a gem can produce shades of green, red, brown, yellow, blue, or black. Chromium gives rise to tints of green, violet, red, and yellow. Manganese, titanium, uranium, and several other elements are among the coloring agents. Thus, the gemstone beryl may occur as blue-green (aquamarine), as pink (morganite), as rich green (emerald), as yellow (golden beryl), or even colorless (goshenite).

Gemstones such as beryl and sapphire that depend on impurities for their color are said to be *allochromatic;* others, such as peridot and garnet, which are highly colored even when pure, are said to be *idiochromatic.* The color of a gem is further described according to its *hue, tint,* and *intensity.* Hue refers to the kind of color, such as red, yellow, green, etc.; tint refers to the lightness or darkness of the hue; and intensity refers to vividness or dullness. Throughout history, the most popular colored stones have been those with hues of red, green, or blue of dark tint and high intensity.

The effect of a gem on light may be more than the production of color. Several of the so-called phenomenal stones are prized for other effects. Holes, bubbles, and foreign particles, when properly aligned in parallel groupings, can produce interesting light

The 138.7-carat Rosser Reeves Star Ruby not only has excellent color but remarkable asterism, resulting from light reflection of three sets of needlelike inclusions arrayed at 60-degree angles to each other.

effects. The play of colors of opal and labradorite, the *chatoyancy* or silky sheen of tiger's-eye and cat's-eye, the *opalescence* or pearly reflections of opal and moonstone, and the *asterism* or star effect of rubies and sapphires are caused by the reaction of light to accumulations of minute *inclusions* or imperfections in the gemstone.

When light passes into or through a gemstone with little or no interruption, the stone is said to be transparent. A stone through which light passes with greater difficulty is said to be either translucent or opaque, depending on the degree of light interruption.

Frequently, the internal structure of a gem acts as a filter, permitting only certain kinds of light to pass through. When all kinds are transmitted, the gem appears white or colorless. Otherwise it assumes the hue of the color transmitted. Strikingly, some gems will transmit different colors depending on the direction light passes through. This phenomenon is known as *pleochroism* and is often quite noticeable in tanzanite, kunzite, and cordierite.

The action of a gemstone upon the light which strikes its surface, and is either reflected or passed through it, sometimes results in other highly desirable effects that enhance its beauty and aid in its identification. Light passing into a stone is bent from its path, and the amount of bending (*refraction*) depends upon the species of the gemstone. When the degree of bending can be measured, the gem species can be identified, since very few species of gemstones bend light to exactly the same degree. An instrument called a gem refractometer is used to determine the degree to which cut stones refract, or bend, light. The measurement obtained is the *refractive index* of the gemstone.

Many gemstones can split a beam of light and bend one part more than the other, thus producing *double refraction*, or two different measurements of refractive index.

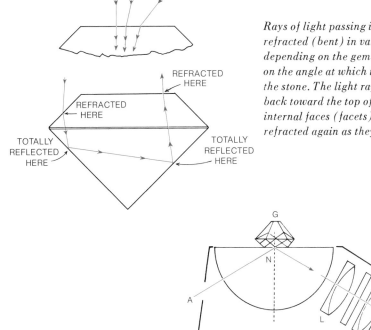

REFRACTED HERE

REFRACTED HERE

TOTALLY REFLECTED HERE

TOTALLY REFLECTED HERE

Rays of light passing into a gemstone are refracted (bent) in varying amounts depending on the gem species and also on the angle at which the light strikes the stone. The light rays are reflected back toward the top of the stone by internal faces (facets), and they are refracted again as they leave.

A gem refractometer is a simple device used to measure quickly the refractive index of a cut gemstone. When a beam of light is passed through the opening (A), it is reflected from the table of a gemstone (G) through a lens system (L) and, by prism (P), into the eye of the observer (E). The maximum angle of reflection (N), which depends on the refractive index of the gemstone, controls the angle at which the beam comes through the eyepiece (EP). The refractive index is read directly from a scale in the eyepiece.

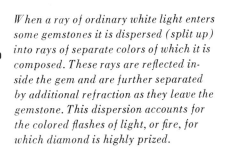

white light   violet   red

DISPERSION

When a ray of ordinary white light enters some gemstones it is dispersed (split up) into rays of separate colors of which it is composed. These rays are reflected inside the gem and are further separated by additional refraction as they leave the gemstone. This dispersion accounts for the colored flashes of light, or fire, for which diamond is highly prized.

Gems have the ability to separate "white light" (the mixture of all colors) into its various colors, producing flashes of red, yellow, green, and other colors. Separation occurs because the various colors, or wavelengths composing white light passing through the gem, are each bent or refracted a different amount. Red is bent least, followed in order by orange, yellow, green, blue, and violet, which is bent most. This characteristic of being able to produce flashes of color, as seen prominently in diamond, is known as *dispersion* or *fire*. Quartz and glass have low dispersion, and hence they make poor diamond substitutes. Some of the newer synthetic gemstones, such as titania, have extremely high dispersion, with resulting fire. Zircon, a natural gemstone of suitable hardness, exhibits high dispersion and is a commonly used substitute for diamond.

Since gems are embraced in the mineral kingdom, and minerals are naturally occuring chemical substances, it follows that all the accepted terms of chemical description can be applied to them. When a chemist learns that ruby is an impure aluminum oxide, he understands a great deal about the nature, origin, and behavior of ruby. He can assign to it the chemical formula Al_2O_3, symbolizing its basic composition as two atoms of aluminum united with three of oxygen. Similarly, other popular gemstones can be described chemically as follows:

Diamond	Carbon	C
Sapphire	Aluminum oxide	Al_2O_3
Quartz	Silicon dioxide	SiO_2
Emerald	Beryllium aluminum silicate	$Be_3Al_2(SiO_3)_6$
Spinel	Magnesium aluminate	$Mg(AlO_2)_2$

Significantly, ruby and sapphire are chemically identical, both being of the mineral species corundum. As already explained, the difference in color is due entirely to very slight traces of chemical impurities. Frequently, the impurities are present in irregular patches that give spotty color effects.

Some mineral species possess many of the desirable qualities of gemstones yet cannot be used as gems because they are chemically active and therefore are less durable. They undergo alteration and decomposition when exposed to light or to one or another of such substances as air, water, skin acids, and oils. With very few exceptions all the better known gems are mineral oxides or silicates. A few oxides, such as corundum, chryso-beryl, and spinel, are remarkably durable. Most silicates—substances containing the elements silicon and oxygen in their compositions—are, on the other hand, generally resistant to alteration and decomposition, unlike the sulfides, carbonates, and most other mineral groups. One notable exception to the rule is carbon, which occurs as the extremely durable diamond.

The Shaping of Gemstones

Gemstone crystals often have naturally brilliant, reflecting faces, but rarely are they perfect and unblemished. Also, their natural shapes do not provide the best expression of their luster, brilliance, dispersion, color, and other inherent properties. In fashioning a gemstone, the skilled artisan tries to develop these hidden assets and to otherwise enhance the gemstone's general beauty.

From ancient times until the 1600s little was attempted in the way of shaping gemstones other than to smooth or polish the natural form. Although similarly smoothed, or *tumbled*, gemstones recently have returned to fashion, the finest pieces of gem rough are now converted mainly into *faceted*, or shaped, stones. Standard types of facets—the flat faces that are ground and polished on the rough gem material—have been given individual and group names. A typical example is the *brilliant* cut, which is most commonly used to best bring out the qualities of a diamond.

The diagram shows a brilliant-cut diamond with angles and facets arranged to give the stone maximum internal reflection as well as to make use of its strong dispersive ability. Certain of the light beams passing into a brilliant-cut diamond produce colorless brilliance by being reflected back out of the stone through the *table* by which they entered. Other light beams, emerging through inclined facets, are split up by dispersion into the rainbow, or fire, effect so prized in diamonds. A stone that has been cut too wide for its depth, with incorrect facet angles, will look large for its weight but its brilliance and fire will have been drastically reduced.

For other purposes and for other kinds of precious stones a number of basic cuts have been developed. The *brilliant* and *step* cuts are by far the commonest of these basic cuts,

The standard brilliant cut, with a pattern of many facets, is commonly used for gemstones having a high refractive index and, therefore, great brilliance.

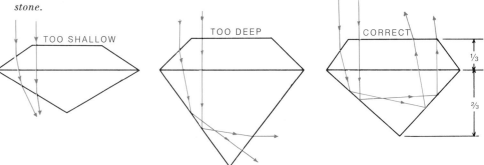

Ideal proportions for the standard brilliant cut have been carefully determined so that the maximum amount of light will be reflected back out the top of the stone. Incorrect proportions cause the light to be lost at the bottom of the stone.

Characteristic of the standard brilliant cut are the 32 crown facets surrounding a relatively small, flat, table facet and the 24 pavilion facets and culet at the bottom of the stone.

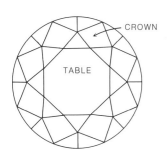

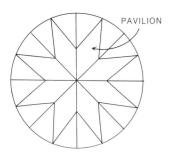

but modern jewelry design frequently uses such fancy cuts as the baguette, cut-corner triangle, epaulet, half moon, hexagon, keystone, kite, lozenge, marquise, pentagon, square, trapeze, and triangle. Some of these are shown here.

In general, there are three operations in preparing a gemstone from the rough—sawing, grinding, and polishing. Sawing usually is accomplished by using a thin, diamond-impregnated, rapidly rotating disk of soft iron or bronze, with oil or water being used as a coolant. The very hard diamond dust literally scratches its way through the stone. Once the stone is sawed to shape, the facets are ground and polished on a rotating horizontal disk by the use of various abrasives. For rough grinding, silicon carbide—or sometimes diamond powder—is used. Scratches are removed and a high polish is given by the use of tin oxide, pumice, rouge, or other fine-grained abrasives. The thick disks, or *laps*, are made of cast iron, copper, lead, pewter, wood, cloth, leather, and certain other materials. Since each species of gemstone differs in its characteristics, each must be treated somewhat differently as to sawing and lapping speeds, kind of lap, and choice of abrasives. Because of the greatly increased interest in gem cutting as a hobby and the large number of amateur cutters, a substantial market has developed in the United States for lapidary supplies and equipment. New kinds of machinery, new abrasives, and new kinds of saws and laps are introduced regularly. Fundamentally, however, the process still involves sawing, grinding, and polishing.

Shaping of gemstones is not limited to geometric faceting. Many stones, especially those which are opaque or which produce stars and cat's-eyes, are cut as *cabochons*. This ancient, and probably oldest, cutting style consists merely of a raised and rounded form. When extended completely around the stone, the cabochon form results in a bead that can be drilled and strung. Many cabochons, especially those of less expensive gem materials, are now cut in large quantities to standard sizes in order to fit mass-produced gem mountings.

Sculpting in gemstones is a much more intricate, nongeometric kind of shaping. Although tools differ in detail, and the gem sculptor must possess an artistic eye as well as lapidary skill, the basic processes of sawing, grinding, and polishing are the same.

16

The step cut (left), often called the emerald cut, frequently is used for colored stones because the large table permits a good view of the color.

The emerald or step cut (below) provides a large table and a full bottom for the stone. Although the number of crown facets and pavilion facets may vary, the general pattern is maintained.

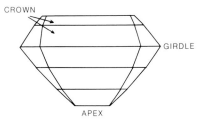

CROWN

GIRDLE

APEX

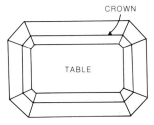

CROWN

TABLE

The simplified English brilliant cut (left) takes maximum advantage of the strong dispersion of diamond, with its flashes of fire, but the fewer facets provide less sparkle than the standard brilliant cut.

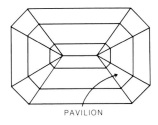

PAVILION

The English brilliant cut (below) has 28 crown and pavilion facets—28 fewer than the standard brilliant cut.

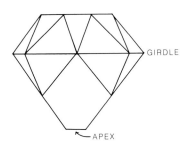

GIRDLE

APEX

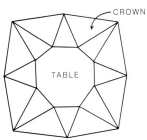

CROWN

TABLE

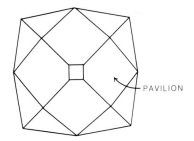

PAVILION

Various kinds of cuts have been devised for special purposes in jewelry design. These include the pentagon (1), lozenge (2), hexagon (3), cut-corner triangle (4), kite (5), keystone (6), epaulet (7), baguette (8), trapeze (9), and square (10).

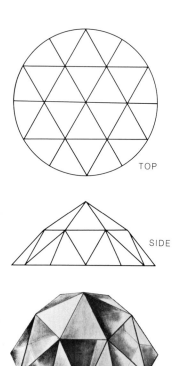

TOP

SIDE

The Dutch rose cut is a very simple one that is used mainly for small diamonds in jewelry that features a larger, colored stone. It is based on a form that originated in India and was introduced through Venice.

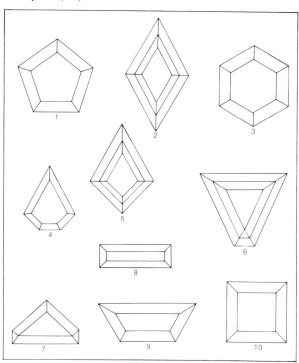

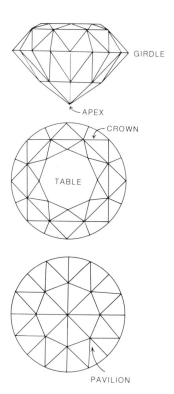

GIRDLE

APEX

CROWN

TABLE

PAVILION

The step brilliant cut is a complicated modification of the standard brilliant. With an additional 12 facets in the crown and 8 in the pavilion, the step brilliant has 78 facets compared with the 58 of the standard.

Just as the English brilliant cut, because of its 28 fewer facets, has less sparkle than the standard brilliant cut, the step brilliant, with its 20 additional facets, has greater sparkle.

Cutting a star stone requires careful attention to the directions in which the cuts are to be made. Failure to align the stone properly with the axis of the crystal will produce a stone with an off-center, crooked, or dim star, or may even eliminate the star completely.

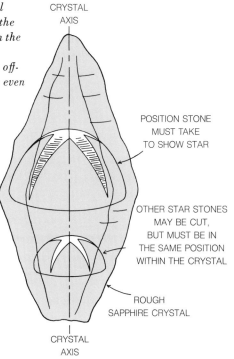

CRYSTAL AXIS

POSITION STONE MUST TAKE TO SHOW STAR

OTHER STAR STONES MAY BE CUT, BUT MUST BE IN THE SAME POSITION WITHIN THE CRYSTAL

ROUGH SAPPHIRE CRYSTAL

CRYSTAL AXIS

Thin-walled, 8- and 12-inch agate bowls carefully cut by craftsmen of the centuries-old carving center at Idar-Oberstein, Germany.

The world-famed crystal ball, given to the collection as a memorial to W. R. Warner by his widow, represents another phase of the lapidary art. Cut from a block of Burmese quartz estimated to have weighed 1000 pounds, this extremely valuable, flawless, colorless sphere has a diameter of $12\frac{7}{8}$ inches and weighs $106\frac{3}{4}$ pounds.

19

A 2-foot ivory piece carved in China from a fossil mammoth tusk. Part of the design was required to remove parts of the tusk that had decomposed through the ages.

Ornate, assembled carving making good use of the colors of carnelian, amethyst, garnet, and other minerals for the realistic fruit, and serpentine for the leaves.

The coral carving at left, 11 inches tall without the stand, and its companion at right owe their graceful, willowy form to the skill of the artist in following the contour of natural coral branches. Center carving is typical of those done in one of the many synthetic substitutes for amber.

The cabochon cut gets its name from the French word "caboche," meaning pate or knob, a reference to the rounded top of the stone. Here, from top to bottom, beginning at left, are cabochons of turquoise, agate, and petrified wood; jasper, smithsonite, and williamsite; and amazonite, petoskey stone, and carnelian.

21

Gem Substitutes

Because of their rarity and relatively high cost, the number of real gems used throughout recorded time must be insignificant compared to the number of gem substitutes used. There are records of glass and ceramic imitations of gems as early as 3000 B.C. Certainly, the world gem markets today are flooded with substitutes and man-made gems. There even has been developed a laboratory process for growing a coating of synthetic emerald on the surface of a faceted stone of natural colorless beryl. The recut gem looks like a natural emerald, and it has natural inclusions that totally synthetic emeralds lack.

In general, gem substitutes can be classified as imitation stones, assembled stones, reconstructed and altered stones, and synthetic stones.

IMITATION STONES Any material will serve as an imitation of a natural gem as long as it resembles the real thing under casual examination. Because of the great variety in types and colors available, glass and plastics are the most commonly used materials for making imitation gems. Almost every gem has been simulated effectively. The substitutes offer no difficulty of identification to the expert, but many are deceptive to the layman.

ASSEMBLED STONES It has been the practice for centuries to build up gemstones by fusing or cementing a shaped piece of natural gemstone to another piece, or other pieces, of inferior or artificial material.

A colorless common beryl crown cemented to a pavilion of green glass produces an emerald doublet—part natural, part artificial—of good color and high durability. A thin piece of beautifully colored opal cemented to a base of inferior opal provides an assembled stone that looks like a thick piece of high-quality opal. Triplets, and even stones in which there are pockets of colored liquids or metal foil between the shaped pieces, are known.

Usually, assembled stones are easily detected, since the joint will show under magnification, but sometimes they are mounted in settings that obscure the joint, and detection is more difficult.

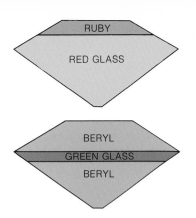

Samples of assembled imitation gemstones. If it were measured on its natural ruby table, the assembled stone at top would have all the characteristics of a large ruby, including refractive index. Since emerald is green beryl, an inexpensive colorless beryl sandwich of green glass (bottom) would appear to be an expensive emerald. The joints of assembled stones often are hidden in the jewelry mountings.

RECONSTRUCTED AND ALTERED STONES

Ruby fragments have been heated at high temperature to partially melt them into a large mass that could be cut into a more valuable stone. Ruby is the only stone that has been somewhat successfully reconstituted in this way, but there are many other ways of tampering with natural stones to make them more desirable.

Sometimes natural stones are backed with foil or a metallic coating to enhance their color, to provide brilliance, or to produce a star effect. It is said that in an inventory of the Russian crown jewels by the Soviet Government, the ruby-colored Paul the First Diamond was discovered to be a pale pink diamond backed by red foil. Today, some diamonds are coated on the back with a blue film to improve their color.

Aquamarine, when pale greenish blue, may be heated in order to deepen the blue color, and poorly colored amethyst may be heated to produce a beautiful yellow-brown quartz, called citrine, that often is misrepresented as topaz. By strong heating, the brown and reddish brown colors of zircon can be changed to blue or colorless, both of which states are unknown in natural zircon. Dyes, plastics, and oils are used to impregnate porous gems such as turquoise and variscite, and even jade. Off-color diamonds, when exposed to strong atomic radiation, can be changed to attractive green, brown, and yellow colors, causing them to resemble higher-priced *fancies.*

In the constant search for something new, gem suppliers sometimes introduce into gemstones colors that are not always an improvement. For example, the beautiful purple of some amethyst can be converted, by heat treatment, to a peculiar green. Such an altered stone is marketed as *greened amethyst.*

All of this tampering with gemstones complicates the problem of identification, so it is a matter of serious concern to the gem trade.

SYNTHETIC STONES

For over 200 years mineralogists have been devising techniques for producing synthetic minerals in the laboratory, and attempts have been made, sometimes with considerable success, to apply these techniques to the production of synthetic gemstones. To qualify as a synthetic gemstone the man-made product must be identical chemically and structurally with its natural counterpart. Sapphire, ruby, spinel, emerald, and rutile in gem quality have been brought to commercial production.

Two of the basic techniques used in producing synthetic gems are the *flame-fusion* and the *hydrothermal* processes.

In the flame-fusion process—invented in 1904 by the French chemist Verneuil—powdered aluminum oxide, containing coloring agents, is sieved down through the flame of

23

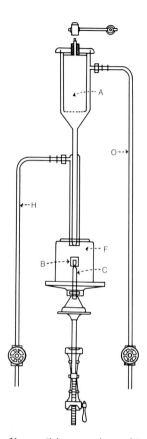

a vertical blowtorch furnace. As it passes through the flame, the powder melts and accumulates as drops on an adjustable stand just below the flame, where it forms a single crystal *boule* of the synthetic rough. In a few hours a boule of several hundred carats can be formed. When such furnaces are operated in banks of several hundred units, the commercial production of corundum alone becomes possible at the rate of many tons a year. Through the years, of course, refinements have been made on Verneuil's original furnace.

In the hydrothermal process, which differs greatly from Verneuil's flame-fusion process, crystals are grown from solutions of the raw materials that have been subjected to varying conditions of very high pressure and temperature. Some of the quartz used for electronics purposes also is manufactured in this way. There are, of course, other processes and numerous synthetics, which may or may not match naturally occurring gemstones.

Synthetic gemstones offer a very serious challenge to those concerned with gem identification when chemical composition and crystal structure—the basic characteristics by which a gemstone is identified—are identical in both the manufactured product and its natural counterpart.

The Verneuil furnace, for making synthetic gem rough. A mixture of hydrogen (H) and oxygen (O) burns almost explosively, heating the fusion chamber (F) to high temperatures. For example, powdered aluminum oxide and coloring agents are sifted down from hopper (A) to the fusion chamber and form a cylindrical boule (B) on an adjustable stand (C).

Gem Lore

All sorts of magic and symbolic properties have been ascribed to gemstones through the ages; for example, the cat's-eye has been prescribed as a cure for paleness, citrine has been worn as a protection from danger, and the opal cherished as the symbol of hope. The result has been the creation of an intricate, chaotic, and contradictory but interesting mass of gem lore.

The Bible describes the jeweled breastplate worn by Aaron, first high priest of the Hebrews. After the destruction of the Temple and its restoration, a second breastplate was made and supposedly was modeled after the one worn by Aaron. As nearly as can be determined, in these plates were mounted twelve stones representing the Twelve Tribes of Israel. Among Christians, the Twelve Apostles also were represented symbolically by precious stones.

THE TWELVE TRIBES	THE TWELVE APOSTLES
Levi, *Garnet*	Peter, *Jasper*
Zebulon, *Diamond*	Andrew, *Sapphire*
Gad, *Amethyst*	James, *Chalcedony*
Benjamin, *Jasper*	John, *Emerald*
Simeon, *Chrysolite*	Philip, *Sardonyx*
Issachar, *Sapphire*	Bartholomew, *Sard*
Naphtali, *Agate*	Matthew, *Chrysolite*
Joseph, *Onyx*	Thomas, *Beryl*
Reuben, *Sard*	James the Less, *Topaz*
Judah, *Emerald*	Jude, *Chrysoprase*
Dan, *Topaz*	Simon, *Hyacinth*
Asher, *Beryl*	Judas, *Amethyst*

The number "12" seems to follow a chain of gemstone superstitions. Gemstones were considered to have mystical relationship not only with the Twelve Tribes and the Twelve Apostles but also with the Twelve Angels, the Twelve Ranks of the Devil, and the Twelve Parts of the human body.

Some stones were even endowed with astrological significance and were believed to be in sympathy with the twelve zodiacal signs. On the basis of an elaborate system of prognostications, an astrologer was considered able to foretell future events by proper observance of changes in hue and brilliance of the symbolic stones.

Aries the Ram, *Bloodstone*	Libra the Scales, *Chrysolite*
Taurus the Bull, *Sapphire*	Scorpio the Scorpion, *Aquamarine*
Gemini the Twins, *Agate*	Sagittarius the Archer, *Topaz*
Cancer the Crab, *Emerald*	Capricornus the Goat, *Ruby*
Leo the Lion, *Onyx*	Aquarius the Water Bearer, *Garnet*
Virgo the Virgin, *Carnelian*	Pisces the Fishes, *Amethyst*

Perhaps in our own space-oriented times the ancient superstitions sympathetically relating certain gemstones with the planets will be revived. In the distant past, moonstone, topaz, and other white stones were believed to be in sympathy with the Moon, diamond and ruby with the Sun, jasper and emerald with Mars, amethyst, topaz, and emerald with Venus, carnelian, topaz, and amethyst with Jupiter, turquoise and sapphire with Saturn, and rock crystal, agate, and emerald with Mercury. Since Uranus, Neptune, and Pluto were unknown to the ancients, these planets have not been represented by gemstones.

Of special interest to the American public are birthstones. Many birthstone lists have been proposed, and in order to use this idea to popularize gemstones the American jewelry industry has agreed upon an official list. This list has served to bring about some uniformity in the selection of birthstones for the twelve months.

January, *Garnet*	July, *Ruby*
February, *Amethyst*	August, *Peridot* or *Sardonyx*
March, *Aquamarine* or *Bloodstone*	September, *Sapphire*
April, *Diamond*	October, *Opal* or *Tourmaline*
May, *Emerald*	November, *Topaz* or *Citrine*
June, *Moonstone* or *Pearl*	December, *Turquoise* or *Lapis lazuli*

All these associations and strange beliefs have served to create in the general public a mental image of gemstones that gives to them an increased exoticism and mysterious appeal far exceeding their monetary value.

Principal Gem Species

An excursion into the literature of gems would reveal that there is much to be discovered about them other than the cold facts of gemology, techniques of gem cutting, and tales of gem lore. When all the information about an individual species is assembled, it provides a sketch of a fascinating gemstone personality. Whole books have been written about diamond—books filled with essays on its mining history, natural occurrences, scientific significance, and best known cut stones.

In the following sections of this book, some of the facts about several of the better known gem species have been gathered. The treatment is not meant to be complete, but enough information is given so that the Museum visitor may better understand and remember what he has seen.

For each species described there are color illustrations of certain gemstones displayed in the collection. Several photographic and artistic techniques have been used to emphasize the various aspects of the beauty of these stones, many of which are the largest and finest of their kinds known; however, not all of the finest gems are pictured here.

At the end of this descriptive section is a list of the significant faceted gemstones in the collection. Obviously, this list will change, because new gemstones constantly are being acquired.

DIAMOND

Diamond is the king of gems. It is a form of pure carbon, and it is the hardest substance known; only diamond will cut diamond. It is interesting that the humble graphite, its close relative, is also pure carbon, but graphite is so soft that it is used as a lubricant and for making the "lead" in pencils.

27

The Hope Diamond, because of its long and dramatic history and its rare deep-blue color, is probably the best known diamond in the world. By speculation, the Hope is linked to the famous "French Blue," which was brought to France from India in 1668 to become part of the crown jewels of Louis XIV. The French Blue was stolen in 1792 and never recovered, but in 1830 an extraordinary 44.5-carat blue diamond—presumably cut from the missing gem—came on the market. It was purchased by Henry Thomas Hope of England and became known by its present name. In 1949 the gem was acquired from the estate of Mrs. Evalyn Walsh McLean by Harry Winston Inc., of New York. Ten years later, this same company presented the gem, in Mrs. McLean's original setting, to the Smithsonian Institution.

The ancients believed diamond to be indestructible, and even today many people believe that diamond cannot be broken. Despite its great hardness, however, diamond is not exceptionally tough, and it can be split along what diamond cutters call its *grain*.

The diamond's high brilliance results from its very high refraction, or ability to bend light, and its fire is caused by its high dispersion, or ability to divide light into its rainbow colors. However, only in properly cut stones are diamond's brilliance and fire developed to their maximum.

At great depths in the crust of the Earth and under conditions of very high pressure and temperature, diamonds form in pipe-like bodies of kimberlite, a heavy dark rock consisting primarily of two minerals, pyroxene and olivine. In South Africa diamonds are mined from the kimberlite, but they also are recovered there and elsewhere from beds of sand and gravel where they have accumulated after being released from their mother rock by erosion.

The world's largest diamond deposits are in Africa, and names such as Congo, Sierra Leone, and the Union of South Africa bring to mind colorful legends of fabulous discoveries of diamond. Smaller deposits are found in South America—in Brazil, British Guiana, and Venezuela—and in Asia. Even in the United States some diamonds have been found.

India was the most important source of diamond until 1728, when discoveries were made in Brazil. Among the important large diamonds found in India were the Koh-i-noor, the Great Mogul, and, very likely, the Hope Diamond. Like India, Brazil in turn declined as a major source of diamond with the discovery and efficient recovery of large quantities in South Africa.

Diamonds are extremely rare even in diamond mines. For example, the famous South African mines contain only one part of diamond in more than 14 million parts of worthless rock. In spite of this, more than three tons of gem- and industrial-quality diamond are mined each year.

Among the British crown jewels is a cut diamond weighing 530.20 carats (more than $3\frac{3}{4}$ ounces), one of several stones that were cut from the largest gem diamond ever dis-

The Eugenie Blue Diamond, an extra-ordinary 31-carat, bright-blue, heart-shaped gem, presented to the Smith-sonian Institution by Marjorie Merri-weather Post.

Magnificent, 12-carat "canary" diamond ring. Such pleasant and strongly colored diamonds are generally more valuable than colorless diamonds of equivalent size and quality.

covered. The rough stone, known as the Cullinan Diamond, weighed 3106 carats (almost 1¾ pounds) when it was found at the Premier Mine in South Africa in 1905. It appeared to have once been just part of a still larger stone.

Diamonds vary from colorless to black and from transparent to opaque. As they come from the mines, they are graded into two groups, gem and industrial. Those whose color, imperfection, or shape make them useless as gems—more than 8 out of every 10 carats mined—are used in industry. Diamonds of industrial quality also are produced synthet-ically, and these are used primarily in the manufacture of grinding wheels.

The best gem diamonds are flawless and are colorless or slightly blue. Their value depends on their color, clarity, cut, and carat weight. Most costly are those called fancies, which have a distinct color such as blue, pink, green, or deep yellow.

PEARL The pearl is included among gemstones only because it is a beautiful object used in jewelry. As has been noted, pearl is not a mineral because it is formed by the action of living organisms. However, the pearl has long occupied an important position among jewels, and it is unique in requiring no lapidary art to enhance its beauty. Nature has perfected pearls.

The ancient Chinese believed that pearls originated in the brain of a dragon. We now know, of course, that pearl is created by a secretion of a mollusk. Very few mollusks have the ability to produce the fine mother-of-pearl used in the jewelry trade, and even among those that can, very few produce pearls with iridescence, or *orient*, as it is known in the trade. Only two genera, the pearl oyster (*Margaritifera*) and the pearl mussel (*Unio*) are important sources of the gem. Edible oysters rarely produce pearls, and when they do, the pearls are of poor quality.

The shells of pearl-producing mollusks are composed of layers of calcium carbonate in the form of either calcite or aragonite. These layers, cemented together with an organic substance known as conchiolin, are known as nacre. The layer closest to the animal is deposited in tiny overlapping patches, producing an iridescent effect caused by the interference of light rays reflected from the plates making up the nacre. The same material coats the surface of a gem pearl.

Seldom does a mollusk live out its time without attack by creatures boring through its shell, or without intrusion through the normal shell opening of tiny parasitic worms, sand, or other irritants. Usually inert particles are forced against the inside of the shell, where they are covered with layers of pearl that fasten them to the shell. This is the source of most *blister pearls*. When the irritant remains in its fleshy part, the mollusk deposits a protective shell of pearl to cover it completely, and a spherical pearl may result. Pearls of less-symmetrical shape, called *baroques*, are more common.

The value of a pearl depends on its shape, color, orient, and size. Pearls of highest value are white with a faint tinge of pink or yellow, possess fine orient, are round, and are free of surface blemishes. The grading of pearls for color requires considerable experience to detect delicate differences. Various classification names, such as "rosée" for delicate pink shades, are used. Fancy colored pearls are those with a strong yellow, bronze, pink, green, blue, or black color. Grading for shapes, which differ markedly, is easier. Spherical pearls are usually drilled for beads; pear-shaped or drop pearls are used in earrings and pendants; and "boutons" or button-shaped pearls, with one flat side, are used for ear ornaments, cuff links, and rings. Irregular, baroque pearls and tiny seed pearls are used in jewelry designs with noble metals and perhaps other gemstones.

The world's finest pearls, called *oriental pearls*, come from the fisheries of the Persian Gulf. Fine pearls also are found off the coasts of Burma, Tahiti, New Guinea, Borneo, Venezuela and western South America, and in the Gulf of California. Fresh-water pearls of high quality, formed in pearl mussels, are found in various rivers in Europe and the United States, especially in rivers in the Mississippi Valley.

A method of growing *cultured pearls* has been well developed. A mother-of-pearl bead is inserted in the oyster as an irritant, and the animal is replaced in the sea in a cage. When oysters so treated are recovered after a period of three to seven years, the beads in

the harvested crop usually are found to be coated with a layer of nacre up to almost a sixteenth of an inch thick.

The cultured pearl can be identified only by the observance—through a drill-hole or by X-ray—of the mother-of-pearl core, which had been inserted in the oyster. An instrument called an endoscope, devised for rapid testing of drilled pearls, relies on a beam of strong light carried by a hollow needle. The needle is inserted into the drill hole, and as it passes through the center portion of a natural pearl a flash of light, reflected through a mirror system in the needle, is observed.

CORUNDUM
RUBY AND SAPPHIRE

Both *ruby* and *sapphire*, which are second only to diamond in hardness, are of the mineral species corundum, an oxide of aluminum. They are identical in all characteristics except color. Most corundum is opaque, and it is mined in large quantities for use as an abrasive. In a few places, such as Moguk in Upper Burma and in Ceylon, clear corundum is found that is suitable for use as a gem.

Red corundum is known as ruby. Its color, caused by traces of chromium, ranges from rose through carmine to a dark purplish red referred to as pigeon's blood red. Rubies of this very desirable latter color often are called Burma rubies, and they are the most costly of all the corundum gems.

All gem corundum having a color other than red is sapphire. The name sapphire means blue, and this is the color most frequently associated with this gemstone. The finest sapphires are a velvety cornflower blue, and they come from Kashmir. Blue, white, yellow, gold, pink, and all the other colors of corundum are caused by the presence of slight traces of iron, chromium, titanium, and other metals present as dissolved impurities in the aluminum oxide. Frequently sapphires are found that show patches of blue and yellow, or that have alternating zones of red and blue. Pure corundum is colorless.

Most gem corundum comes from the Orient, at localities such as Moguk in Upper Burma, near Bangkok in Thailand, Kashmir in India, and Ceylon. The dazzling 423-carat Logan Sapphire, pictured on the cover of this book, is from Ceylon. Because of this primarily Asian origin, the word *oriental* often is used with the names of other gems to denote a sapphire of a particular color. For example, green sapphire sometimes is called oriental emerald, and the yellow sapphire sometimes is called oriental topaz.

A piece of uncut ruby from Burma and five small cut rubies from Ceylon. All have the classic "pigeon's blood" color.

There are some notable exceptions to the generally oriental occurrence of corundum. Some good-quality ruby has been found in North Carolina, and sapphire of many colors has come from Montana.

During the formation of a corundum crystal, extremely small needlelike inclusions of rutile sometimes occur in the hexagonal pattern of the host crystal. When such inclusions are arranged in this way by nature, they cause, in properly cut stones, internal reflections that produce the optical phenomenon known as asterism. The effect is that of a 6-rayed star, and the gems in which asterism occurs are known as star sapphires and star rubies. Asterism is rarer in ruby.

Since corundum is easily manufactured, synthetic ruby and sapphire are used extensively in jewelry. The synthetic stones can be distinguished from natural stones by microscopic examination of the kinds of inclusions and internal defects.

VARIETIES

Ruby: Red
Sapphire: Blue, yellow, pink, green, colorless, and any color except red

Star sapphire: Colored as sapphire and showing asterism
Star ruby: Red and showing asterism

Beryl is one of the most widely used colored gemstones, and under its several names in the gem world it is perhaps the best known. When it is a rich green it is known as *emerald*, and when it is the blue-green of sea water it is called *aquamarine*. Varieties such as the rose-pink *morganite*, golden-yellow *heliodor*, and colorless *goshenite* are less well known than emerald and aquamarine but are equally attractive and satisfactory gemstones.

Beryl is beryllium aluminum silicate. It frequently occurs in well-formed hexagonal crystals, and its many colors result from the presence of very small percentages of several different elements. Emerald owes its rich green color to traces of chromium, and the detection of this element is one of the means of identifying true emerald. Aquamarine, comprising the green and blue-green beryls, gets its color mainly from traces of iron. Practically all of the deep blue aquamarine available in jewelry stores results from the heat treating of greenish beryl or certain yellow-brown beryls. The stones are heated carefully to about 800° F., and the color change is permanent. The element lithium accounts for the color of pink beryl. As with aquamarine, the color of yellow beryl is now considered to be the result of traces of iron rather than uranium, as previously thought. Pure beryl is colorless.

Beryl usually is found in pegmatites, which are very coarse-grained granite rocks formed by the cooling of molten material far beneath the Earth's surface. As the rock cools and beryl and other crystals are formed, the stresses introduced are so great that the crystals frequently shatter so badly they are useless as gem material. Frequently, too, impurities are introduced during crystal formation, and consequently the gem materials are found only where the crystals were able to form without interference—such as in openings or cavities in the rock.

Tremendous beryl crystals weighing as much as several tons, but not of gem quality, have been discovered in a few localities. Large crystals of gem quality also occur in nature, and large cut stones of aquamarine and other colors of beryl are relatively common. Among the fine examples of beryl in the National Gem Collection is a remarkably large (2054-carat), flawless cut stone of rich yellow-green. This gem and others in the collection weighing 1363 carats, 1000 carats, 914 carats, and 578 carats accentuate the occurrence of large gem crystals of beryl in Brazil.

The finest emeralds are not found in pegmatites. At Muzo in Colombia, the most pro-
lific source of the finest emeralds, they occur in veins with calcite, quartz, dolomite, and
pyrite. The veins cut through dark-colored, carbonaceous limestone and shale. Mining at
Muzo began 350 years ago and still continues sporadically to meet market requirements.
Russian emeralds occur as good-sized crystals in mica schist, a metamorphic rock. They
occur there with chrysoberyl, phenakite, and common beryl. Some of the smaller stones
have good color and have been cut into valuable gems. Brazil, which produces many extraordinary aquamarines and other beryls, has not produced quality emeralds. Periodi-
cally, over the centuries, there have been reports of new discoveries of emerald, but so far
none of these has begun to rival the Muzo source in either quantity or quality of the gems
produced.

Although Brazil supplies the finest aquamarine and Colombia the finest emerald, several localities in the United States are sources of good-quality beryl of these colors.
Foremost among these localities are Maine, California, and Connecticut for aquamarine

and North Carolina for emerald. Morganite of pale pink to deep peach color, from California, is also notable. Various New England mines in Maine, New Hampshire, and Connecticut and the gem mines of the Pala and Mesa Grande districts of California have produced other colors of gem beryl. However, most of the beryl mined in the United States is used as an ore for beryllium, as little of it is of gem quality.

Because of its hardness (about 8), vitreous luster, beautiful color, and rarity, emerald always has been highly prized as a gem. Fine-quality emeralds may be more costly than fine diamonds. Other kinds of beryl have the same physical properties as emerald, but since they are less rare their relative value is lower.

Synthetic emerald of high gem quality has been marketed successfully. A synthetic substitute for aquamarine is also available; it is really a synthetic blue spinel.

VARIETIES

Emerald: Grass green
Aquamarine: Blue green
Morganite: Pink

Heliodor: Yellow
Goshenite: Colorless

TOPAZ Because yellow is the most popular color of topaz it has become customary to believe that all topaz is yellow. Also, there is a tendency to believe that all yellow gemstones are topaz. Neither belief is correct. Stones of yellow, sherry, blue, pink, and colorless topaz all make beautiful gems, and their characteristics are identical except for color. On the other hand, citrine (a yellow quartz), although entirely unrelated to topaz, often is disguised in the trade under the names Brazilian topaz, topaz quartz, or just topaz. Great numbers of stones described and sold as yellow topaz really are the much commoner citrine, which has few of the characteristics of fine topaz.

Topaz, an aluminum fluosilicate, has a hardness of 8, a vitreous luster, and a relatively high refractive index. It is found in near-perfect crystals that range in size from very small to very large, with some giants weighing as much as several hundred pounds. Most of these crystals, especially the largest ones, are colorless, a characteristic that indicates relatively high purity of composition. Although topaz gems have little fire, they take a high polish and can be very brilliant. Great care must be taken in cutting and polishing topaz because of its ready cleavage. The desired cut and high polish can be secured by avoiding excessive heat or pressure during the operation and by planning facets so that none lies exactly parallel to the cleavage direction.

Although crystals of gem-quality topaz are found in many localities, perhaps the splendid blue ones from Russia and the yellow, wine, blue, and colorless ones from Brazil are best known. Some fine topaz has been found in the United States in such widely separated areas as New Hampshire, Texas, Colorado, and California. The light, golden brown

A 3273-carat topaz of soft blue that came from Brazil. The Smithsonian Institution had this unique gem cut by John Sinkankas of California. For several years it was the largest topaz in the collection.

Three different cutting styles and colors of topaz. From top, a 235-carat colorless stone from Colorado, a 171-carat dark champagne-colored stone from Madagascar, and a 129-carat sherry-colored stone from Brazil.

topaz from Colorado has an unfortunate tendency to fade in strong sunlight. It remains to be seen whether similar topaz coming recently from comparable occurrences in Mexico also will fade. By a system of heating and cooling, certain of the red-brown topaz crystals from Ouro Preto, Brazil, can be converted to colors ranging from salmon pink to purple red. Quick heating to high temperatures can completely remove color, and sudden or uneven cooling may cloud or crack the stone.

37

OPAL Opal has been admired for its great beauty since ancient times, but this gemstone lacked commercial appeal until the discovery of the Australian black opal late in the 19th century.

Opal is somewhat brittle, is sensitive to heat, and, in some cases, tends to deteriorate despite the best of care. Therefore, this stone lacks many of the physical characteristics required for an ideal gem. These deficiencies would eliminate other species from the list of gemstones, but the great beauty of its flashing and shifting color patterns has made opal increasingly popular. Even its name, coming from the ancient Sanskrit "upala," means precious stone.

With a hardness between 5½ and 6½, opal is the softest of the more popular gems. It is sufficiently hard, however, to be used in jewelry, where its setting usually helps to protect it from shock and abrasion.

Opal is unlike most gemstones in that its flashing color is not due to the color of the stone itself, or even to the color of its included impurities. Rather, it is due to the way in which tiny opal particles are grouped during its formation. Detailed photographs taken through an electron microscope show clearly how precious opal is deposited as spheres so small that they are indistinguishable under powerful optical microscopes. These spheres are packed together in very orderly networks, row upon row and layer upon layer, with tiny open spaces, also in rows, between them. Masses of common opal lack this orderly internal arrangement of spheres. White light striking the precious opal is reflected independently by each row of spheres, much like the reflections from a series of slats in a venetian blind. Since these rows of spheres are spaced at distances approximately the same as the wavelength of light, a phenomenon known as *diffraction* occurs. The separate reflections interfere with each other in an organized manner, cancelling out some of the light wavelengths and reinforcing others, producing color. The brilliant color flashes are of different hues depending on the sizes of the spheres of opal and, therefore, the distances between rows. To provide the best display of this optical effect, opal is almost always cut in cabochon form rather than as faceted stones.

Common opal, which shows milky opalescence, does not exhibit color flashes, and it is not used as a gemstone. Each of the common varieties—such as hyalite, cacholong, and hydrophane—has its own slightly different set of characteristics, but only precious opal, with its dazzling color display, is important for gem purposes. To take full advantage of the small amounts of gem material available, or to bring out its color better, *precious* opal is often cut as thin pieces and mounted as doublets on some other backing. Also, the seams in rock sometimes are cut so that the thin layer is exposed on a thicker backing of the adjoining rock. Precious opal, or gem opal, is classified as *white opal* when the color flashes are in a whitish or light background, *black opal* when the background material is gray, blue-gray, or black, and *fire opal* when the background is more translucent and red, reddish orange, or reddish yellow.

Precious opal has been found in several areas of the world—in nodules, in seams in rock, or as replacements of other minerals or even of wood and shell. Hungarian deposits were well known in Roman times, but these and other deposits became insignificant with

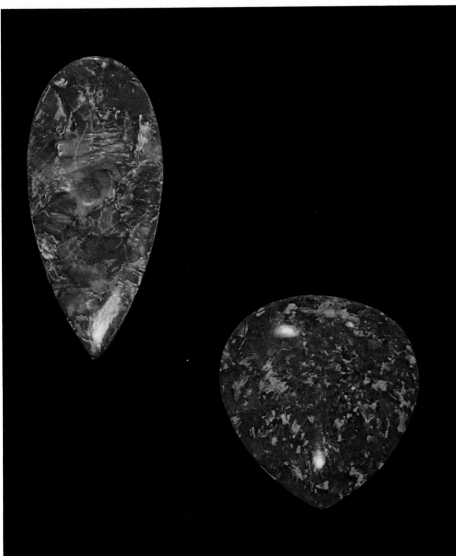

Black opal, so called because the color flashes appear against a dark background, is found in Australia. It is quite rare, and large pieces, such as the 1-inch cabochon on the right, have become extremely valuable.

These fire opals have a strong play of colors. Some fire opals have background colors that vary from bright yellow through orange and red, but some are colorless. Stones such as the ones shown below, which weigh 7, 11, and 22 carats, have made Querétaro, Mexico, famous as their source.

the discovery of opal in Australia in the late 19th century. Opal deposits were discovered in 1889 at White Cliffs in New South Wales, and other important discoveries in Australia followed, including deposits at Lightning Ridge in New South Wales that produce very dark stones and the rich fields of white opal at Coober Pedy in South Australia. Mexico has remained for a long time the principal source of richly colored fire opals, with the most important deposits located in the state of Querétaro, where mines have been worked intermittently since 1835. This has made the town of Querétaro today the center for the trade and cutting of Mexican opal.

VARIETIES

White opal: Color flashes in light-colored background material
Black opal: Color flashes in dark gray or bluish background material
Fire opal: Orange or reddish background material

39

SPINEL

The ideal and much-coveted red color in spinel is displayed by this 8.7-carat gem, a gift of Mr. and Mrs. James H. Clark. Similarity to ruby color has given this type the popular name of "ruby spinel."

Two of the more famous stones in the British crown jewels are the Black Prince's Ruby and the Timur Ruby, but neither of these stones is really ruby. Like many gems long thought to be ruby, these two British stones are spinel. Although spinel occurs in many colors, such as yellow, green, violet, brown, and black, it is the red spinel that usually is seen in the gem trade. There are several varieties of red spinel, such as *ruby spinel, balas ruby, rubicelle,* and *almandine spinel*—all of which refer to the color resemblance to ruby.

Spinel is an oxide of magnesium and aluminum, and it is not related to ruby. However, because its hardness (8) is only slightly less than that of ruby and its brilliance is about equal to that of ruby, spinel makes an excellent substitute for that gem. Also, because it is more plentiful, spinel costs much less. It is interesting that red spinel, like ruby, gets its color from the presence of traces of chromium.

Synthetic blue spinel is widely used as a substitute for aquamarine, and synthetic spinels of other colors are used as substitutes for many gems. However, the synthetic stones are not ordinarily made in the subtle shade so characteristic of natural spinel. Completely colorless spinel apparently exists only as a synthetic material. Actually, because of its hardness, durability, and many attractive colors, spinel makes a fine gemstone in its own right.

Like ruby and several other gemstones, spinel is found chiefly in the gem gravels of Ceylon, Burma, and Thailand. Appreciable amounts of spinel occur in the Ceylon gem gravels as worn, rounded pebbles of many colors. In the Burmese gravel deposits, the spinel is often found as well-formed octahedral crystals. Near Moguk, in Burma, spinel has been found in its original position in the limestone rocks as well as in the eroded stream deposits.

VARIETIES

Almandine spinel: Purplish red
Rubicelle: Orange-red
Balas ruby: Rose red
Ruby spinel: Deep red
Chlorospinel: Translucent grass green

Ceylonite or pleonaste: Opaque dark green, brown, or black
Picotite or chrome spinel: Translucent dark yellow-brown or green-brown

40

Few gemstones can compete with quartz for variety of color. Having a hardness of 7 and occurring in many beautiful varieties, only the relative abundance of quartz prevents the species from attaining top rank among gemstones.

The two kinds of quartz, crystalline and cryptocrystalline (fine-grained) quartz, occur in all kinds of mineral deposits throughout the world. Much of this material is suitable for cutting gems.

Colorless crystalline quartz, or *rock crystal*, makes attractive faceted gems, and it is used as a suitable substitute for diamond and zircon even though it lacks the fire and brilliance of those gemstones. Some very large, flawless crystals of colorless crystalline quartz have been found. The great Warner Crystal Ball, with a diameter of $12\frac{7}{8}$ inches and weighing $106\frac{3}{4}$ pounds, was cut from such a crystal. Another unusual gem in the quartz collection is the faceted quartz egg (see frontispiece). In addition to the name rock crystal, colorless crystalline quartz appears in the jewelry trade under such names as rhinestone (not to be confused with the glass substitute), Herkimer diamond (from Herkimer County, N. Y.), and Cape May diamond (from Cape May, N. J.).

The most popular variety of quartz is *amethyst*, a transparent form whose color ranges from pale violet to deep purple. In many cut stones of amethyst the color intensity changes sharply from section to section. This is due to irregular color zoning common to amethyst crystals. The actual cause of the purple color in amethyst is not very well understood. There are fewer cut stones of amethyst in very large sizes because of the rarity of large, flawless, well-colored crystals.

QUARTZ
INCLUDES ROCK CRYSTAL, AMETHYST, AND CITRINE

A 783-carat step-cut citrine of deep, rich color dwarfs a 278-carat brilliant-cut citrine (at left), a 90-carat smoky quartz, and a 91-carat briolette of citrine. The smoky quartz, from Switzerland, is so dark that it appears to be opaque. The other three stones came from Brazil. The briolette and brilliant-cut citrines were cut and donated to the Smithsonian Institution by Albert R. Cutter.

All of the gems in this spread are varieties of quartz in several of its most attractive and popular colors from amethyst to rose to golden.

The name *citrine* (from the French word for lemon) attempts to describe the yellow color of another variety of quartz. Actually, the normal coloring of citrine varies from yellow to red-orange and red-brown, but the yellow sometimes rivals the yellow of topaz. In addition to the normal color range, the colors of citrine may grade through a grayish yellow variety known as *cairngorm* and a grayish variety called *smoky quartz* to a black variety called *morion*. Other varieties that add color dimensions to the group of quartz gemstones are *rose quartz* and *milky quartz*. Like amethyst, the reason for the color in rose quartz has not been definitely established. Milky quartz owes its color to myriads of tiny cavities containing water or liquid carbon dioxide.

The range of color in quartz is somewhat surprising, considering that the mineral is a simple silicon dioxide. Some of the colors, as with corundum and some other gemstones, are due to traces of impurities. In quartz, these consist mainly of oxides of iron, manganese, and titanium. However, all the reasons for quartz coloration in its many varieties are not known.

In addition to possessing wide variation of color, quartz, like sapphire and certain other gemstones, can exhibit asterism or chatoyancy. The well-known *tiger's-eye* from West Griqualand, South Africa, owes its eye effect to the fact that its material is a replacement of fibrous asbestos by cryptocrystalline quartz. The color of tiger's-eye arises from the partial alteration of the asbestos to yellow-brown iron oxides before it is replaced by quartz. Inclusions of rutile, tourmaline, or actinolite needles may produce attractive patterns in quartz, but they do not always cause chatoyancy. The material containing such inclusions is called sagenitic quartz, or it may be descriptively named, such as rutilated quartz, tourmalinated quartz, and so forth. Sagenitic quartz is usually cut as cabochons rather than as faceted stones since the inclusions are of greater interest than the quartz itself.

If the foreign inclusions consist of tiny flakes of hematite or mica, the quartz assumes a spangled appearance and is called *aventurine*.

Crystals of quartz varieties that are opaque or that contain visible inclusions normally are cut as cabochons to take advantage of the body color or to make the inclusions more visible. Crystals of the transparent varieties are fashioned in any of several cutting styles, depending on whether it is desired to take maximum advantage of color or of brilliance. Because of its availability in fairly large, flawless pieces in various colors, quartz has been used extensively in carving. The Chinese have excelled in carving large, ornate objects of rock crystal.

Although quartz occurs in many varieties and its crystals are cut in many styles, it is easily identified by its refractive index of 1.55, specific gravity of 2.65, and hardness of 7.

This modern-day snuff bottle of Australian chrysoprase with a ruby-crystal stopper was carved by Mrs. Helen Hanke.

CRYSTALLINE VARIETIES

Amethyst: Purple to violet
Cairngorm: Smoky yellow
Citrine: Yellow to red-orange and red-brown
Milky quartz: White

Morion: Black
Rock crystal: Colorless
Rose quartz: Rose to pink
Smoky quartz: Gray to black

CRYPTOCRYSTALLINE VARIETIES (CHALCEDONY)

Agate: Pronounced color banding
Aventurine: Inclusions of sparkling flakes
Bloodstone: Dark green dotted with red
Carnelian: Red to yellow-red
Cat's-eye: Chatoyant
Chrysoprase: Green

Jasper: Opaque brown to red-brown, green, yellow, etc.
Onyx: Color banding in straight layers of contrasting color
Sard: Light to dark brown
Sardonyx: Sard or carnelian bands alternating with white bands
Tiger's-eye: Bright brownish yellow, sometimes blue; chatoyant

CHRYSOBERYL
INCLUDES ALEXANDRITE
AND CAT'S-EYE

With color ranging from shades of yellow and brown through blue-green to olive, and with a hardness of 8½, chrysoberyl has most of the characteristics necessary for a fine gem. Rare stones of high-quality chrysoberyl demand fairly high prices, and they are sought eagerly by the connoisseur of gemstones.

Chrysoberyl is beryllium aluminate, and thus is closely related to the gemstone spinel, which is magnesium aluminate. When pure, chrysoberyl is colorless and relatively uninteresting as a gemstone because of its lack of color dispersion and its moderate refractive index of 1.75. However, few pure samples are known, as chrysoberyl normally contains some iron or chromium in place of aluminum and some iron in place of beryllium. As a result of such impurities, the color of chrysoberyl may be yellowish, green, or brownish.

Chrysoberyl and beryl are the only important gemstones containing the element beryllium. The minerals beryllonite, euclase, hambergite, and phenakite also contain this element, but they are rare and seldom are seen as cut gems.

The *alexandrite* variety of chrysoberyl has two colors in delicate balance, and it changes from a columbine red to an emerald green when viewed under different light.

43

In addition to its fine cat's-eyes and its color-changing alexandrite varieties, chrysoberyl occurs in handsome stones that vary considerably in color. Shown here with an uncut twinned crystal of gem quality from Brazil—gift of Bernard T. Rocca, Sr.—are a 46-carat stone from Brazil (left) and a 121-carat stone from Ceylon.

One of the finest-quality chrysoberyl cat's-eyes in existence is the 58-carat Maharani from Ceylon.

When viewed in daylight, which is richer in green, the color balance shifts toward green, and that hue is seen by the observer. Under artificial light, normally richer in red, the color balance shifts toward red, and the stone seems to have changed to that color. This extremely rare stone, named after Czar Alexander II of Russia, is found only occasionally, primarily in Russia and Ceylon. The Russians stones, found with emerald in mica schist, tend to be smaller than the Ceylon stones and have a color change going from emerald green to violet-red. The Ceylon stones, found as pebbles in gem gravels, have a color change going from a less-emerald green to a browner red. The 66-carat, record-size alexandrite in the National Collection shows the color change typical of Ceylon stones. A synthetic stone is commonly marketed as synthetic alexandrite, but this substitute not only is man-made but is actually synthetic corundum instead of synthetic chrysoberyl.

Cat's-eye chrysoberyl contains myriads of tiny fiberlike channels arranged in parallel position. When the stone is cut as a cabochon, a band of light is reflected from the curved top of the stone, producing an effect that resembles the slit pupil of a cat's-eye.

VARIETIES

Alexandrite: Green in daylight, changing to red in artificial light

Cat's-eye: Chatoyant

Because of its great color range, which includes pink, green, blue, yellow, brown, and black in many different shades and combinations of shades, tourmaline is one of the most popular of the colored gemstones. Tourmaline with a color near emerald green is particularly popular.

Chemically, tourmaline is a very complex borosilicate, and its color is determined by the various elements present in it. Tourmaline crystals having sodium, lithium, or potassium are either colorless, red, or green; those having iron are blue, blue-green, or black; and those having magnesium are colorless, yellow-brown, or blackish brown.

Some crystals of tourmaline are of two colors, and stones of mixed colors, such as pink and green, can be cut from these. The color mixing may show as zoning with the core color of the crystal overlaid by another color and perhaps even additional layers of other colors. Zoned crystals with a core of deep pink covered by a layer of green have been called "watermelon tourmaline." Because its refractive index of about 1.6 is too low to give it marked brilliance, and its color dispersion is too low to give it fire, the tourmaline relies almost solely on the beauty of its color for its rank in popularity.

Although tourmaline has a low refractive index and low dispersion, it exhibits remarkable dichroism. In other words, it can present different tints to the viewer depending on the direction that the light is traveling through the crystal. When viewed down the long, or vertical, axis of the crystal, the color of tourmaline is much stronger than when viewed from the side. This means that if the crystal is dark the cutter will have to cut the stone with the flat part, or table, parallel to the long axis of the crystal. The color of the gemstone then will be lightened when viewed from its table, since this is the direction of lighter color. Similarly, the table of a lighter-colored crystal can be cut perpendicular to the long axis in order to produce a deeper-colored gem.

TOURMALINE

Weighing 28.2 carats, this heart-shaped gem of the red or rubellite variety of tourmaline is from Brazil and was a gift of Mr. and Mrs. James H. Clark.

Green seems to be the best known commercial color of tourmaline, but this extremely variable gem species exhibits many subtle color blends such as those shown here. At upper left, a 104-carat stone from Mozambique; at upper right, a 173-carat stone from Mozambique; at lower left, a 111-carat stone from Manchuria; and at lower right a 35-carat stone from Brazil.

Some tourmaline crystals contain threadlike tubes of inclusions of microscopic size running parallel to the length. When cut as cabochons, such crystals give a good "cat's-eye" effect.

Tourmaline has no distinct cleavage and has a hardness somewhat above 7, and these characteristics make the stone efficiently resistant to normal shock and wear so that it is highly satisfactory for use in jewelry.

Noted deposits of tourmaline are located in the Ural Mountains of Russia, Ceylon, Burma, South-West Africa, Madagascar, Brazil, Maine, and California. Crystals from each of these localities seem to have their own color specialties. The deposits in San Diego County, Calif., are unique in that all colors except brown are found there. In the early 1900s pink and red tourmaline was shipped from there to China for carving, but this thriving trade stopped with the end of Chinese imperial reign. The tourmaline deposits at Paris, Auburn, and Hebron, Maine, have furnished a number of excellent gems, especially of blue and green colors.

VARIETIES

Achroite: Colorless   *Dravite:* Brown
Indicolite: Blue   *Schorl:* Black
                               Rubellite: Pink

ZIRCON Zircon, because of its high refractive index and high dispersion, approaches diamond in degree of brilliance and fire. On only casual examination it is quite possible to mistake a well-cut, colorless zircon for a diamond. However, a careful examination of the back facets of such a stone, when viewed through the table, would show strong double refraction, a characteristic of zircon but not of diamond. Zircon's double refraction makes the back facet edges appear doubled. Since diamond is "singly refracting," it cannot produce this double appearance of the back facets.

Zircon is brittle and has a hardness of just over 7, while diamond's hardness, as we have seen, is rated at 10. After being worn in jewelry for a long period of time, zircon will show signs of chipping on the facet edges. Under the same conditions, diamond would remain unchanged. Because of this tendency for facet edges to chip, it is the practice in the gem trade to pack cut zircons separately. If a number of zircons were placed in the same paper packet there would be a risk of "paper wear."

In the gem trade, the most important zircons are those that are colorless, golden brown, or sky blue. Such stones originally were reddish brown zircon pebbles from Indochina, but they have been converted by being subjected to temperatures approaching 1800° F. for periods of up to two hours. When the original zircons are heated in a closed container, the stones become blue or colorless; when a flow of air is allowed through the container, the stones become golden yellow, red, or colorless. In most of these converted stones the

The beautiful colors of these brilliant zircons are the result of heat treatment given to natural, reddish-brown stream pebbles. The three stones at the left (from top) weigh 118, 103, and 98 carats, and the ones on the right weigh 106 and 29 carats. The 106-carat stone came from Thailand, the two blues from Indochina, the others from Ceylon.

color remains quite stable, but in some it may revert to an unattractive greenish or brownish blue after a period of time.

In addition to being reddish brown, natural zircon may vary from almost colorless to yellow, red, orange, and brown or from yellow-green to dark green and, occasionally, blue.

The most important producing areas of gem zircon are in a region of Indochina that comprises parts of Thailand, Viet Nam, and Laos. Additional gem zircon, like so many of the other gem species, is recovered from near Moguk in Upper Burma and from the gem gravels of Ceylon.

There is no synthetic zircon on the market, but a bright blue synthetic spinel is sometimes used to simulate zircon successfully.

PERIDOT

The relative rarity of peridot and the ease with which it can be simulated in glass, whose luster it approximates, probably account for the low popular demand for this gemstone. Although peridot has little brilliance and no fire, its unusual color and glassy luster produce a unique effect that serves to make it attractive.

The color of peridot is an unusual bottle green that shades, in some stones, toward yellow-green and, more rarely, toward brown. In 1952 it was discovered that almost all of the brown gems believed to have been peridot in various gem collections were actually of an entirely unrelated species, which since has been named sinhalite. Brown peridot still remains rare and is somewhat of a collector's item.

The green of peridot, which is quite different from the green of other gemstones, is due to some iron included in its composition. It is suspected that a trace of nickel contributes to the liveliness of the color.

Peridot has a hardness of only 6½ and a rather strong tendency to cleave, and these

47

characteristics reduce its value for use in jewelry exposed to rough wear. It is better used in pins, earrings, and pendants than in rings.

Peridot is a gem name for the common mineral olivine, a magnesium silicate. Olivine is found in numerous places, and small gemmy pieces are found in many localities. Many of the largest and best gems of peridot have come from mines on the Egyptian island of Zebirget (Island of St. John) in the Red Sea, but most gem peridot now comes from Burma. Great numbers of small stones have been cut from olivine found in Arizona gravels.

Centuries ago, peridot was known by the name topaz, since the stones came from Topazos, the island now known as Zebirget. The name topaz, as we have seen, is used today for an entirely different mineral species.

SPODUMENE

Spodumene, a lithium aluminum silicate, is one of the very few gemstones containing lithium. It has had more importance as a gemstone in the United States than elsewhere, a situation due to early discoveries of unique occurrences of a lavender-pink variety at Branchville, Conn., in 1879 and in San Diego County, Calif., about 20 years later. At the time of the discovery of the California material, the variety was named *kunzite* in honor of G. F. Kunz, a noted American gemologist of the times.

The finding of a bright green variety, *hiddenite,* in North Carolina about 1880 greatly stimulated the interest of American gem collectors. Some of the bright green spodumene coming from Brazil in recent years compares very favorably in color with North Carolina hiddenite. Other than in a scattered few of these unusual occurrences of kunzite and hiddenite, spodumene usually is found in yellow and yellow-green shades, with Brazil and Madagascar being the chief sources.

Spodumene has a hardness of about 7, but with a refractive index of about 1.66 and a low dispersion there seems to be relatively little to recommend it as a gemstone. The fact that it exhibits a very strong tendency to cleave in two different directions would seem to rule it out completely as being too difficult to cut. Nevertheless, the production and purchase of cut stones of spodumene persist because of the beauty of the gem.

The kunzite and hiddenite varieties of spodumene show strong *pleochroism,* or the ability to show three different colors when viewed in the direction of different axes. Some of the large Brazilian kunzite crystals mined in the early 1960s have an intense rose-violet color when viewed along the long axis of the crystal but have pale blue-violet and pale tan colors when viewed from the other two directions. When heat-treated, or exposed to strong light, this Brazilian kunzite loses its tan and bluish colors but retains the intense rose-violet. Because of spodumene's pleochroism, the direction of cutting in the stones becomes extremely important, as it must be done in a manner that will take advantage of the violet color in kunzite and the green color in hiddenite.

VARIETIES

Kunzite: Lavender violet to rose violet   *Hiddenite:* Deep green

48

Its 880-carat size makes this one of the largest kunzite gems known. Remarkably, it is also practically flawless.

Many of the larger and better-quality stones of spodumene, usually in shades of green and yellow green, come from Brazil. This square-cut 69-carat gem is a fine example.

GARNET   The name garnet is applied to a group of six closely related silicate minerals that are alike in crystal structure but that differ mainly in the substitution of certain metallic elements in their composition. These minerals are:

Pyrope, magnesium aluminum garnet   *Uvarovite*, calcium chromium garnet
Almandine, iron aluminum garnet   *Grossular*, calcium aluminum garnet
Spessartine, manganese aluminum garnet   *Andradite*, calcium iron garnet

Most natural garnets have compositions intermediate between members of the basic group of six. For example, there are garnets having compositions anywhere between pyrope and almandine, depending on the amount of difference in the magnesium or iron content. These same garnets may even have varying amounts of manganese, and thus be partially spessartine.

The six garnets in the basic group are found in considerable quantity in many areas, but seldom are they of sufficiently high quality to be considered gemstone material. Even when stones of gem quality are found, their colors—particularly the reds— tend to be so intense that they seem to be opaque.

Garnet has a hardness (about 7) suitable for gemstone material and a fairly high refractive index (1.74 and above).

Ruby red pyrope is the most popular variety of garnet. It is found in Bohemia, Czechoslovakia, where it occurs as small, poorly shaped crystals. Red pyrope also is found in Africa, where it is called Cape ruby, and in Arizona, where it is sold as Arizona ruby. Another kind of pyrope called *rhodolite* is noted for its soft, rosy purple color. Actually, rhodolite is one of the intermixed garnets with a composition somewhere between pyrope and almandine. Many of the fine rhodolite gems have come from North Carolina.

Almandine is popular in its deep red, transparent form, but since the red is so dark and intense that it appears black, the stones usually are cut as cabochons with the back hollowed out. This makes them thinner, and thus lightens their color. Garnets cut in this manner are all known as carbuncles. Brazil, India, Ceylon, Australia, and parts of the United States are important sources of almandine.

Although spessartine has a rich orange color, it is not often used as a gemstone because of the relative rarity of gem-quality cutting material. This mineral gets its name from the town of Spessart, Germany, where it was first found. Excellent spessartine with colors ranging from orange to brown has been found at Amelia Court House, Va., and quality gems have been cut from such material. Ceylon, Burma, Madagascar, and Brazil also have furnished some gem spessartine.

The chromium garnet, uvarovite, generally is too poor in quality for cutting. Uvarovite crystals, which are emerald green in color, occur in only small sizes. They are found mostly in Russia, Finland, and California.

Grossular varies in color. It occurs chiefly in some shade of red, green, yellow, or brown, depending on the impurities present. When pure, grossular is colorless. A kind of grossular called *hessonite* has an attractive cinnamon color, and it is found mainly in Ceylon. Because of its color it can easily be confused with spessartine, which it closely resembles.

Andradite, a very common garnet, usually is found in shades of red, black, brown, yellow, or green. Some types of gem andradite have special names for different colors:

topazolite, yellow; *demantoid*, green; and *melanite*, sparkling black. The very valuable demantoid is found in Russia and Italy.

The name jade is applied to two unrelated minerals—*nephrite* and *jadeite*—that have **JADE** somewhat similar characteristics.

Jadeite, the rarer of the two, is a sodium aluminum silicate that belongs to a group of rock-forming minerals known as pyroxenes. Its color varies from white to emerald green and many other colors. Jadeite is highly prized, and when it occurs as emerald green it is considered one of the most valuable gemstones. This kind of jade is found in many places, but the most important occurrence is in Upper Burma. Nephrite, a more common species, is a calcium magnesium iron silicate belonging to a group of rock-forming minerals known as amphiboles. The color varies from white to a dark spinach green and black. Among the places where nephrite occurs are New Zealand, Turkestan, Siberia, Alaska, China, Silesia, and certain parts of the western United States, notably in Wyoming and California.

Jade is not particularly hard ($6\frac{1}{2}$), but it is very tough, and this characteristic makes it an excellent material for carving. Even when subjected to punishing usage, jade resists chipping and wear. It was used for making tools and weapons by primitive peoples who lived in what is now Mexico, Switzerland, France, Greece, Egypt, Asia Minor, and in other places. The jade implements fashioned by these peoples have survived well the ravages of time.

The Chinese and Japanese prize jade highly. In their countries, tradition has assigned to jade medicinal and spiritual values, and has associated with it the cardinal virtues of charity, modesty, courage, justice, and wisdom. As a consequence, these peoples long ago developed the carving of jade as a high art. Among the magnificent Chinese jade carvings in the National Gem Collection are 130 pieces produced mostly during the Ching Dynasty (1644-1912), when the art of jade carving was at its peak. Many of these jades were carved in imitation of the revered bronze ceremonial vessels of ancient times. This collection was presented to the Smithsonian Institution in 1959 by Mr. Edmund C. Monell in behalf of the estate of his mother, Mrs. Maude Monell Vetlesen of New York.

*Jade carving 10 inches tall recently cut
in China from Burmese jade. The quality
of the work and excellent use of color
variations in the jade testify to the
vitality of an ancient Chinese craft.*

Obviously, from the appearance of this carved bracelet and the cabochons, jade occurs in several other colors in addition to the traditional greens.

Selections from the Maude Monell Vetlesen collection of Ching Dynasty (1644-1912) jadeite and nephrite jade carvings in the Smithsonian Institution. For size comparison, two cylindrical scroll holders are approximately 1 foot tall.

A Ch'ien Lung period (1736-1795) snuff bottle of jadeite jade with rubellite tourmaline top—a gift of Mrs. Mildred Taber Keally.

CHARACTERISTICS OF SOME COMMON GEMS

Species	hardness	Approximate average of specific gravity	refractive index	Dispersion	Durability	Usual color range
Beryl	7¾	2.70	1.58	Low	High	Green (emerald), blue-green (aquamarine), pink (morganite), colorless (goshenite)
Chrysoberyl	8½	3.71	1.75	Low	High	Yellow, green, brown
Corundum	9	4.00	1.77	Low	High	Red (ruby), various (sapphire)
Diamond	10	3.52	2.42	High	High	Colorless
Garnet group	7½	3.70–4.16	1.74–1.89	Medium to high	High	Yellow, red, green, brown
Jade (nephrite)	6½	2.96	1.62	None	High	Green, white
Jade (jadeite)	7	3.33	1.66	None	High	Green, white
Opal	6	2.10	1.45	None	Low	Red, dark gray, orange, white, with or without varicolored fire
Pearl	3½	2.71	None	None	Low	White
Peridot	6½	3.34	1.68	Low	Medium	Yellow-green, brownish green
Quartz	7	2.65	1.55	Low	High	Purple (amethyst), yellow (citrine), colorless (rock crystal)
Spinel	8	3.60	1.72	Low	High	Shades of red, green, blue, violet
Spodumene	7	3.18	1.66	Low	Low	Colorless, pink, yellow, green
Topaz	8	3.54	1.63	Low	Medium	Colorless, sherry, pink, blue
Tourmaline	7	3.06	1.63	Low	High	Wide range, except bright red
Zircon	7	4.02	1.81	High	High	Almost colorless, blue, brown, green, yellow

A number of mineral species have produced cut gemstones that fulfill every necessary requirement of beauty, durability, and rarity, but their popularity and commercial success have been sharply limited because of insufficient supply. In some cases of even adequate supply such gemstones do not compete with other, more plentiful kinds that exhibit the same characteristics. The scarcity of these minerals does not diminish their standing as potential gem material—it merely points up the effect of accidental natural distribution of these species.

Among the rarer minerals that produce good gemstones are cordierite, benitoite, euclase, phenakite, beryllonite, willemite, wernerite, danburite, datolite, axinite, brazilianite, andalusite, sillimanite, kyanite, kornerupine, enstatite, diopside, epidote, sphene, sinhalite, and orthoclase. Willemite, a rare zinc silicate found in only a few localities, is typical of these rarer minerals. The famous zinc mines at Franklin, N.J., produced a few large gemmy crystals of willemite, and some fine gemstones were cut from some of these. Willemite's borderline hardness of 5 to 5½ and its extreme rarity effectively eliminate it from the gem market, but the collector who is able to obtain a good stone of this material is indeed fortunate.

Some mineral species, although beautiful when cut, and prized by collectors, are entirely too soft, are too easily cleaved, or have some other physical weakness that renders them useless as commercial gemstones. Sphalerite, apatite, fluorite, calcite, cerussite, zincite, and hematite are included in this group. Sphalerite is typical; it produces brilliant and colorful gemstones that hold their own among other stones of great beauty. Unfortunately, this zinc sulfide, with a hardness of 3½ to 4, is so soft and cleaves so readily that it is very difficult to cut properly, and it cannot be used in jewelry.

GEMSTONES FOR THE COLLECTOR

Left: a record-size, 122.7-carat gem of tanzanite from near Arusha, Tanzania. This gem variety of a relatively unattractive mineral species named zoisite was only discovered in recent years.

Right: Since it is so soft and cleaves so easily, sphalerite is seldom well cut as a gem even when suitable pieces are available. This 60-carat stone from Franklin, New Jersey, was cut by John Sinkankas.

This unusual, beautifully colored, high-quality 24-carat gem of labradorite from Oregon was cut by Leon Agee. Most gem cutters are more familiar with the opaque labradorite that has a play of blue color due to its schiller.

A magnificent set of 16 matched sphenes from Switzerland, gift of Nina Lea, almost encircles a 110-carat sinhalite (a rare magnesium borate) and a 22-carat kornerupine, both from Ceylon. The man's gold ring indicates the sizes of these unusual stones.

Gems

in

the

Collection

The Smithsonian's collection of gems continues to grow and improve rapidly, and it changes character constantly as important new gemstones are added and less important ones are retired. A sampling of significant gems currently in the collection is itemized in the following list. Included are some of the largest gems of each kind, some of the more interesting stones, and some small gems notable for the places from which they came. Though listed by species and size, some of the largest stones are not included, and neither are most cabochons, rough opal, beads, carvings, and spheres.

The descriptions listed include, in order, *weight in carats; color; popular name or other description, if any; place of origin; U.S. National Museum catalog number; and name of donor*. Gems in the Lea and Roebling collections usually are indicated by the letters "L" and "R".

DIAMOND

127	colorless (the Portuguese), Brazil, *3898*
44.5	blue (the Hope), India, *3551, Winston*
31	blue (Eugenie Blue Diamond), South Africa, *4863, Post*
29.3	colorless, South Africa, *4220, Riggs*
18.3	yellow (the Shephard), South Africa, *3406*
12	yellow, South Africa, *4668, James*
11.3	yellow, South Africa, *4653, Kellmer*
9	black, South Africa, *R6567, R*
2.9	pink, Tanzania, *3772, DeYoung*

CORUNDUM—Ruby

138.7	red (the Rosser Reeves Ruby, a star), Ceylon, *4257, Reeves*
50.3	red-violet (a star), Ceylon, *173, L*
33.8	red (a star), Ceylon, *1922, L*

CORUNDUM—Sapphire

423	blue (the Logan Sapphire), Ceylon, *3703, Logan*
330	blue (Star of Asia), Burma, *3688*
316	blue (Star of Artaban), Ceylon, *2231, Ingram*
98.6	blue (the Bismarck Sapphire), Ceylon, *4753, Bismarck*
92.6	yellow, Burma, *3549*
67	black (a star), Thailand, *4375, L*
62	black (a star), Australia, *4657, Cutter*
52	yellow, Burma, *3419*
42.2	purple, Ceylon, *4371, Clark*
39.8	blue (a star), Ceylon, *174, L*
35.4	yellow-brown, Ceylon, *2147, L*
31.4	blue, Ceylon, *1027, Shepard*
31	orange, Ceylon, *4357, Clark*
27.4	violet, Ceylon, *4370, Clark*
25.9	yellow, Ceylon, *4194*
25.7	gray (a star), Ceylon, *3902*
25.3	colorless, Ceylon, *2016, L*
24.7	blue (4-starred), Ceylon, *3923, Krandall*
22.4	yellow-orange, Ceylon, *3875, L*
19.9	pink, Ceylon, *4372, Clark*
17.7	pale violet, Ceylon, *2139, L*
16.8	green, Burma, *2172, L*
15.7	colorless, Ceylon, *3581, L*
15.1	pale orange, Ceylon, *3106, L*
12.8	pink, Ceylon, *4373, Clark*

BERYL—Emerald

117	green, Colombia, *4158, Erickson*
27	green, Colombia, *3922*
20	green, Colombia, *4661, James*
17	green, *3920, MacVeagh*
10.6	green, North Carolina, *3704*
7.1	green, North Carolina, *3075, L*
6.5	green, North Carolina, *3076, L*
4.6	green (a cat's eye), Colombia, *2256, R*

BERYL— Aquamarine

1000	blue-green ("Most Precious"), Brazil, *3889, Langer*
911	blue, Brazil, *4348*
263.5	blue, Russia, *3606, Neal*
187	blue, Brazil, *3683*
126	blue, Brazil, *4159, Erickson*
73.2	blue, Brazil, *3982*
71.2	pale blue, Ceylon, *3172, L*
66.3	pale blue-green, Maine, *2148, L*
60.7	blue, Brazil, *2182*
60	blue, Brazil, *4877, Morris*
52.1	pale blue, Brazil, *1874, L*
45	blue, Brazil, *3343*
20.7	pale blue, Madagascar, *1872, L*
15.3	blue-green, Idaho, *2249, Montgomery*
14.3	blue, Connecticut, *779*

BERYL—Morganite

287.3	pink, Brazil, *4618, Trumbull*
235.5	pink, Brazil, *3780, Ix*
178	pink, California, *4286, L*
122.2	pale pink, California, *1988, L*
113	peach, California, *4286, L*
79.6	pale pink, Brazil, *4190, R*
64.1	pink, Brazil, *3721, R*
56	pink, Madagascar, *2223, R*
51	pink, Brazil, *3623*
45.6	pink, Brazil, *3289, L*
37.6	pink, Brazil, *4191, R*
26.9	pink, Brazil, *3302, R*
24.8	pink, Madagascar, *1976, L*
20.2	pink, Brazil, *2225, R*

BERYL—Other Colors

2054	green-gold, Brazil, *3725, R*
1363	green, Brazil, *3916*
914	green, Brazil, *3919*
578	green, Brazil, *3227, R*
133.5	yellow, Madagascar, *1977, L*
113.9	yellow-green, Brazil, *2245, R*
98.4	pale green, Brazil, *3949, Cutter*
61.9	colorless, Brazil, *3366*
46.4	gold, Madagascar, *2121, L*
43.5	gold (a cat's eye), Madagascar, *3248*
40.7	colorless, Brazil
40.4	pale green, Connecticut, *1037, L*
39.6	yellow-green, North Carolina, *2260, R*
23	green, Maine, *1031, L*
19.8	brown (a star), Brazil, *3355, L*
17.5	yellow, Russia, *714, L*
12.3	colorless, Russia, *696, L*
9.7	colorless, New Hampshire, *3340, L*

TOPAZ

7725	yellow, Brazil, *3976*	
3273	blue, Brazil, *3633*	
2680	colorless, Brazil, *4290, L*	
1469	yellow-green, Brazil, *3891*	
685	pale blue, Brazil, *3003*	
398	pale blue, Russia, *3400, R*	
234.6	colorless, Colorado, *3309, L*	
187.2	colorless, Brazil, *3612, Cutter*	
170.8	champagne, Madagascar, *3890*	
155.5	blue, Russia, *262, L*	
146.4	pale blue, Texas, *3625, L*	
129	sherry, Brazil, *3550*	
93.6	orange, Brazil, *3401, R*	
54.4	blue, Brazil, *2219, L*	
50.8	colorless, Japan, *268*	
43.7	blue, Maine, *2047, L*	
43.5	colorless, Brazil, *2.55, L*	
41.4	orange, Brazil, *2.74, L*	
34.1	gold, Brazil, *2046, L*	
34.1	deep pink, Brazil, *2232, L*	
24.4	pale blue, New Hampshire, *3307, L*	
18.1	colorless, Japan, *1178, L*	
18	rose pink, Brazil, *3402, R*	
17.8	colorless, Colorado, *319, L*	
17	blue, California, *3679, Ware*	
14.6	sherry, Colorado, *318, L*	

TOURMALINE—Rubellite

110.8	pink, Manchuria, *3173, R*
62.4	pink, Brazil, *3411, R*
50.5	magenta, Brazil, *4160, Erickson*
35.3	pink, Brazil, *2254, R*
32.4	deep magenta, Brazil, *2252, R*
30	pink, Madagascar, *3409, R*
29.7	pink, Brazil, *2190*
28.2	red, Brazil, *4358, Clark*
19.2	rose, Brazil, *2143*
18.8	rose, Madagascar, *4196, L*
18.4	pink, Maine, *1109, L*
17.5	pink (a cat's eye), California, *3786, L*
16.5	red, Brazil, *4361, Clark*
15.9	rose, Madagascar, *2135, L*
15	rose, Madagascar, *2122, L*
14.5	pink, California, *3412, R*

TOURMALINE—Other Colors

172.7	champagne, Mozambique, *3590, R*
124.8	champagne, Mozambique, *3576, R*
122.9	green, Mozambique, *3575, R*
117	light green, Brazil, *4349*
110	green, Brazil, *4197*
103.9	rose, Mozambique, *3256, L*

76	dark green (a cat's eye), Brazil, *3599, L*
60	blue-green, Brazil, *3410, R*
58.5	green, Maine, *1108, L*
53.2	green (a cat's eye), Brazil, *3119, L*
48	red and green, California, *3363*
41.7	yellow, Brazil, *2251, R*
41.6	brown, Ceylon, *3245, L*
40.3	red-brown, Brazil, *2097, R*
40.3	green, Madagascar, *4081, R*
34.3	red-brown, Brazil, *2253, R*
33.8	rose-brown, Brazil, *3418, R*
31.7	pale green, Brazil, *3414, R*
31.3	rose brown, Brazil, *3416, R*
25.5	blue, Brazil, *3298, R*
23.5	pale brown, Brazil, *3417, R*
21.1	yellow-green, Maine, *4621, L*
20.4	blue-green, Madagascar, *2032, L*
18	green, Brazil, *2142, L*
17.9	green, South Africa, *2095, L*
17.8	brown, Brazil, *2154, L*
17.7	yellow-green, Elba, *3368, R*
17	green, Maine, *1955, L*
15.1	pale green, Brazil, *3413, R*
14.7	yellow, Brazil, *3415, R*

SPINEL

45.8	pale purple, Ceylon, *2180, L*
36.1	indigo, Burma, *3685*
34	red, Burma, *3354, L*
30	violet, Burma, *3344, L*
29.7	pink-violet, Ceylon, *2165, L*
25.5	blue gray, Burma, *3593, L*
22.2	rose brown, Ceylon, *2166, L*
22.1	blue violet, Ceylon, *2247, R*
13.7	mauve, Ceylon, *2138, L*
10.2	red, Burma, *2141, L*
8.69	red, Burma, *4359, Clark*
6.6	(a star), Ceylon, *2255, R*

ZIRCON

118.1	brown, Ceylon, *2236, R*
105.9	brown, Thailand, *3568*
103.2	blue, Indochina, *2222, R*
97.6	yellow brown, Ceylon, *2237, R*
75.8	red brown, Burma, *3068, L*
64.2	brown, Indochina, *3397, R*
51.3	brown, Ceylon, *1179, L*
48.2	colorless, Ceylon, *3554, L*
43.9	pale brown, Ceylon, *2235, R*
29.2	blue, Indochina, *3394, R*
28.1	brown, Thailand, *2173, L*
23.9	colorless, Ceylon, *2234, R*
23.5	green, Ceylon, *2233, R*

22.4	brown, Indochina, *2224, R*	
21.1	tan, Australia, *1887, L*	
10.9	blue, Thailand, *1861, L*	

SPODUMENE—Kunzite

880	deep violet, Brazil, *3940*
336.2	deep violet, Brazil, *3942, Nelson*
296.8	deep violet, Brazil, *3941, Nelson*
177	violet, California, *3797, American Gem Society*
75.9	pale pink, California, *1914, L*
63	pale pink, Brazil, *3684*
60.7	pale pink, California, *1915*
36.3	pale pink, California, *3226, R*
24.7	pale violet, Madagascar, *1979, L*
11.6	pale pink, North Carolina, *3395, R*

SPODUMENE—Other Colors

327	yellow, Brazil, *3396 R*
255.8	yellow, Brazil, *3429, R*
71.1	yellow, Madagascar, *3698, L*
68.8	yellow green, Brazil, *3885, R*
44.9	yellow, Brazil, *2163, L*
24.7	yellow, Madagascar, *2261, C*

PERIDOT

310	olive green, Egypt, *3398, R*
287	olive green, Burma, *3705*
45.5	olive green, Egypt, *1978, L*
22.9	olive green, Arizona, *3620, L*
18.5	olive green, Egypt, *554*
10.4	green, Egypt, *1924, L*
8.9	olive green, Arizona, *1925, L*
8.6	green, Arizona, *3339, L*

GARNET—Almandine

174	red (a star), Idaho, *3670*
67.3	red brown (a star), Idaho, *3560, L*
40.6	red brown, Madagascar, *2137, L*
25.7	red brown, Idaho, *3423, L*

GARNET—Demantoid

10.4	green, Russia, *2175*
4.1	green, Russia, *2150, L*
3.4	green, Russia, *3627*
2.3	green, Russia, *141, L*

GARNET—Grossular

64.2	orange brown, Ceylon, *493, L*
9.2	yellow orange, Ceylon, *2246, R*

GARNET—Rhodolite

22.1	rose violet, Tanzania, *4080, L*
6.4	violet, North Carolina, *460, L*

GARNET—Spessartine

109	red, Brazil, *4203*
53.8	red, Brazil, *3229, L*
40.1	orange, Virginia, *147, L*
26.3	orange, Virginia, *3597, L*
11.8	orange, Virginia, *152, L*

QUARTZ—Amethyst

1362	purple, Brazil, *3879*
202.5	pale lavender, North Carolina, *1286, L*
182.6	purple, Brazil, *1272, L*
61.9	purple, Brazil, *3162, Capps*
61.4	purple, Brazil, *3914, Cutter*
56	purple, Brazil, *3165, Capps*
53.7	purple, Pennsylvania, *1299, L '*
44.5	pale purple, North Carolina, *1298, L*
41.2	purple, Brazil, *4355, Clark*
36.2	purple, Pennsylvania, *1283, L*
33.2	pale purple, North Carolina, *1288, L*
29.7	purple, Brazil, *3166, Capps*
27.5	purple, North Carolina, *1289, L*
26.5	purple, Arizona *3291, R*
22.9	purple, Maine, *1271, L*
22.6	purple, Brazil, *4356, Clark*
21	purple, North Carolina, *1300, L*
18.7	purple, Virginia, *1301, L*

QUARTZ—Citrine

1180	golden brown, Brazil, *1870, L*
783	light golden brown, Brazil, *3640*
277.9	golden brown, Brazil, *3732, Cutter*
264.8	light golden brown, Brazil, *2041, R*
226.9	pale yellow, Brazil, *3718, Cutter*
217.5	golden brown, Brazil, *4199, Cutter*
169	golden brown, Australia, *1373, L*
143.3	yellow, Colorado, *456, L*
120.3	golden brown, Brazil, *2116, L*
155.7	yellow brown, Brazil, *1311, L*
136.3	yellow brown, North Carolina, *1333, L*
114.6	golden brown, Brazil, *3932*
99.7	pale yellow, Ceylon, *1372, L*
97	pale yellow, Ceylon, *1344, L*
95.6	yellow brown, Brazil, *2193*
90.5	yellow, Brazil, *3615, Cutter*
78.8	pale yellow, Brazil, *3621, Cutter*
69.5	yellow, Brazil, *4288, Hurlbut*

55	light golden brown, Maine, *2178, L*
48.4	yellow, Brazil, *3915, Cutter*
42.8	yellow, Brazil, *3719, Cutter*
47.2	yellow brown, Brazil, *2275*
43	yellow brown, Brazil, *2270*
34.4	yellow brown, Brazil, *2276*
21.3	yellow brown, Brazil, *2117, L*

QUARTZ—Rock Crystal

7000	colorless, Brazil, *3957, R*
625	colorless (a star), New Hampshire, *3125, Burroughs*
357.9	colorless, Brazil, *4205, Int. Imp. Co.*
355.6	colorless, Brazil, *4204, Int. Imp. Co.*
353.6	colorless, North Carolina, *1397, L*
350.1	colorless, North Carolina, *1398, L*

QUARTZ—Rose Quartz

625	pink (a star sphere), Brazil, *4264, Hueber*
375	pink, Brazil, *3592, L*
84	pink, Brazil, *3421*
48.8	pink, Brazil, *3420, R*
46.4	pink, Brazil, *3336*
30.4	pink, Brazil, *4807, Mitchell*
21.8	pink, South Dakota, *4510, Jameson*
18.4	pink, France, *1266*
10	pink, South Dakota, *3722, L*

QUARTZ—Smoky Quartz

4500	pale smoky, California, *3738, L*
1695	smoky, Brazil, *3697, L*
785	pale smoky, Colorado, *1335, L*
543	pale smoky, North Carolina, *1339, L*
284.1	pale smoky, North Carolina, *1340, L*
268.5	pale smoky, Switzerland, *1348, L*
163.4	pale smoky, Colorado, *1336, L*
144.9	smoky, Scotland, *3079, R*
128	smoky, Ceylon, *1343, L*
90	dark smoky, Switzerland, *3293*
80	smoky, Arkansas, *1334, L*
63	light smoky, Maine, *1338*
35.1	smoky, Scotland, *1374, L*
32	smoky, New Hampshire, *3124, Burroughs*
20.7	pale smoky, Ceylon, *1347, L*

QUARTZ—Greened Amethyst

22.3	green, Brazil, *3296, L*

CHRYSOBERYL—Alexandrite

65.7	green to red, Ceylon, *2042, L*
16.7	green to red, Ceylon, *3407, R*
11	green to red, Ceylon, *2200, Walcott*

CHRYSOBERYL—Other Colors

171.5	gray green (a cat's eye), Ceylon, *3924*
114.3	yellow green, Ceylon, *4874*
120.5	green, Ceylon, *3001, R*
58.2	green (the Maharani, a cat's eye), Ceylon, *3642*
46.3	green yellow, Brazil, *1923, L*
31.7	brown, Ceylon, *2151, L*
6.7	(a star), Brazil, *3680, Ware*

OPAL

345	white with fire, Australia, *4585, Everhart*
155	white with fire, Australia, *3285, R*
143.2	orange with fire, Mexico, *3968*
83	white with fire, Australia, *3300, R*
58.8	black with fire, Australia, *3960, R*
55.9	colorless with fire, Mexico, *2240, R*
54.3	black with fire, Australia, *3962, R*
44	black with fire, Australia, *3284, R*
39	pale yellow orange with fire, Brazil, *3637*
38.3	black with fire, Australia, *3961, R*
30.1	black with fire, Australia, *3405, R*
24.3	black with fire, Australia, *1897, L*
22	orange with fire, Mexico, *2106, L*
21.8	orange with fire, Mexico, *2028, L*
21.4	yellow with fire, Mexico, *2111, L*
15	orange with fire, Mexico, *2096, L*
11.5	orange with fire, Mexico, *3886, Lewis*

OTHER, LESS-KNOWN SPECIES

AMBLYGONITE
62.5	yellow, Brazil, *4079, L*
19.7	yellow, Burma, *3562, R*

ANDALUSITE
28.3	brown, Brazil, *3619, Kennedy*
13.5	green brown, Brazil, *3364, L*

APATITE
29	yellow, Mexico, *3594, L*
28.8	yellow green, Burma, *3247, L*
19.8	yellow, Mexico, *3570*
14.7	colorless, Burma, *3720, R*
13.9	yellow, Mexico, *2218*
9	yellow green, Canada, *3122, R*
8.8	pale blue, Ceylon, *3639*
7.7	colorless, California, *3636*
5.4	green, Madagascar, *3676, Durand*

AXINITE
23.6	brown, Mexico, *4289, R*
9.4	brown, Mexico, *3787, R*
9	brown, Mexico, *3773, L*
1.6	brown, France, *581*

BARITE
60.7   colorless, England, *3349*

BENITOITE
7.6   blue, California, *3387, R*
1.0   blue, California, *4174, L*

BERYLLONITE
5   colorless, Maine, *423*
3.9   colorless, Maine, *424, L*

BRAZILIANITE
41.9   yellow, Brazil, *3083, L*
17   yellow, Brazil, *3788, R*

CALCITE
75.8   gold brown, Mexico, *4583, R*
45.8   gold brown, Mexico, *3305*

CASSITERITE
10   yellow brown, Bolivia, *3250*

CERUSSITE
4.7   pale yellow, Southwest Africa, *3234, R*

COBALTOCALCITE
3.3, 3.9   pink, Spain, *3724, L*

CORDIERITE
15.6   blue, Ceylon, *3882*
10.2   indigo, Ceylon, *3580, L*
9.4   blue, Ceylon, *3881*

DANBURITE
18.4   yellow, Burma, *3345, L*
7.9   colorless, Japan, *3081, L*
6.4   colorless, Japan, *3074, D'Ascenzo*

DATOLITE
5.4   colorless, Massachusetts, *3876, Boucot*
5   colorless, Massachusetts, *3283, Sinkankas*

DIOPSIDE
133   black (a star), India, *3977*
24.1   black (a cat's eye), India, *3956, L*
19.2   green, Madagascar, *4504, R*
15.5   green, Madagascar, *4505, R*
14   black (a cat's eye), India, *3880*
11.3   green, Madagascar, *2264, R*
10   black (a star), India, *4353, Int. Imp. Co.*
6.8   yellow, Italy, *3634*
4.6   yellow, Burma, *3346, L*
2.2   pale green, New York, *572, L*
1.6   green (chrome diopside), Finland, *3693*

ENSTATITE
11   brown, Ceylon, *3638*
8.1   brown, Ceylon, *2294, R*

EPIDOTE
3.9   brown, Austria, *579*

EUCLASE
12.5   green, Brazil, *3214, R*
8.9   yellow, Brazil, *3215, R*
8.9   yellow, Brazil, *2181, L*
3.7   blue green, Brazil, *3388, R*

FLUORITE
354   pale yellow, Illinois, *3877*
124.5   green, New Hampshire, *3294*
117   green, Africa, *2153*
111.2   violet, Illinois, *4270*
104.3   yellow, Illinois, *4269*
85.4   blue, Illinois, *4875*
63   yellow, Illinois, *3595, L*
32.7   colorless, Illinois, *3626*
17.5   yellow, Illinois, *3635*
13   pink, Switzerland, *4434, C*
8.5   pink, Switzerland, *3730, R*

FRIEDELITE
11.8   red brown, New Jersey, *3013, D'Ascenzo*

GADOLINITE
8.6   black, Texas, *587, L*

IDOCRASE
3.5   brown, Italy, *4179, R*

KYANITE
10.7   blue, Brazil, *3557, L*
9.1   green, Brazil, *3558, L*
4.9   blue, Tanzania, *4508, L*
3.7   blue, North Carolina, *364, Bowman*

KORNERUPINE
21.6   brown, Ceylon, *3706, L*
10.8   brown, Madagascar, *3567, L*
8.1   green brown, Ceylon, *3390, R*
7.6   green, Madagascar, *3782*

LABRADORITE
23.8   pale yellow, Oregon, *4377, L*
11.1   pale yellow, Utah, *3121*
5.8   pale yellow, Nevada, *2155, L*

MICROLITE
3.7   brown, Virginia, *3588, L*

NATROLITE
1.4   colorless, California, *4352, L*

OLIGOCLASE
6   colorless, North Carolina, *404, L*

ORTHOCLASE

249.6   yellow, Madagascar, *3878*
104.5   pale green (a cat's eye), Ceylon, *3883*
61   yellow, Madagascar, *1838, L*
25.9   gray (a cat's eye), Ceylon, *3579, L*
22.7   white (a star), Ceylon, *3578, L*
18   colorless, Madagascar, *1820, L*
16.4   yellow, Madagascar, *3393, R*

PETALITE

55   colorless, Southwest Africa, *4222, L*
10.7   colorless, Southwest Africa, *3096*

PHENACITE

22.2   colorless, Russia, *3739*
9.9   colorless, Brazil, *2263, R*
6.5   colorless, Russia, *4507, R*
5.2   colorless, Russia, *830, L*

PHOSPHOPHYLLITE

5   green, Bolivia, *3950, R*

POLLUCITE

8.5   colorless, Maine, *2056, L*
7   colorless, Connecticut, *3802, R*

PREHNITE

4.4   yellow green, Scotland, *4376, L*

PROUSTITE

9.9   red, Germany, *4802, L*

RHODIZITE

0.5   colorless, Madagascar, *3219, C*

RHODOCHROSITE

9.5   pink, South Africa, *4189, R*

SAMARSKITE

6.6   black, North Carolina, *588, L*

SCHEELITE

37   colorless, California, *3701, L*
18.7   colorless, California, *3389, R*
15.8   colorless, California, *3591, Montgomery*
12.4   gold, Mexico, *3803, R*

SCORODITE

2.6   purple, Southwest Africa, *3793*

SILLIMANITE

5.9   black (a cat's eye), South Carolina, *3600, L*

SINHALITE

109.8   brown, Ceylon, *3587*
43.5   brown, Ceylon, *3548 L*

SPHALERITE

73.3   yellow brown, Utah, *3556*

68.9   yellow brown, Utah, *3362*
59.5   yellow green, New Jersey, *3874, R*
48   yellow, Mexico, *2167, L*
45.9   yellow, Spain, *3707, L*
18.5   yellow brown, Utah, *3555, L*

SPHENE

0.8-9.3   sixteen stones, gold, Switzerland, *2043, N. Lea*
8.5   brown, New York, *550*
5.6   yellow brown, Mexico, *3290, R*
5.2   yellow brown, Mexico, *3292, L*
4.6   yellow brown, Mexico, *4360, Clark*

STAUROLITE

3   dark red brown, Brazil, *3795*

STIBIOTANTALITE

2.5   brown, Mozambique, *3218, C*

TAAFEITE

5.3   mauve, Ceylon, *4509, Kennedy*

TEKTITE

23   brown, Czechoslovakia, *681, L*

WERNERITE

288   colorless, Burma, *3783*
29.9   colorless, (a cat's eye), Burma, *3301, L*
29   pale yellow, Brazil, *2098, L*
19.7   colorless (a cat's eye), Burma, *3561, Ehrmann*
17.3   pink (a cat's eye), Ceylon, *3238, R*
12.3   pink Burma, *3674, L*
8.2   colorless, Madagascar, *1818, L*

WILLEMITE

11.7   orange yellow, New Jersey, *1898, L*
11.1   orange yellow, New Jersey, *4187, L*

ZINCITE

20.1   red, New Jersey, *3386, R*
12.3   red, New Jersey, *3002, R*

ZOISITE

122.7   blue (tanzanite), Tanzania, *4876*
18.2   blue (tanzanite cat's eye) Tanzania, *4584, L*